Village Cricket

Gerald Howat

Village Cricket

Foreword by John Arlott

DAVID & CHARLES
Newton Abbot London North Pomfret (Vt)

FOR ANNE
whose map-reading made it possible
to find the villages we visited,
and who was such a good companion
on the journeys

Books by the same author include:
From Chatham to Churchill
The Story of Health (with Anne Howat)
Dictionary of World History (ed.)
Documents in European History, 1789-1970
Stuart and Cromwellian Foreign Policy
Who did What (ed.)
Learie Constantine
(The Cricket Society Literary Award, 1975)

British Library Cataloguing in Publication Data
Howat, Gerald Malcolm David
Village cricket.
1. Cricket—England—History
2. Villages—England—History
I. Title
796.358'62'0942 GV928.G7

ISBN 0-7153-7727-2

Library of Congress Cataloguing in
Publication Data 79-56048

Typeset by Trade Linotype Ltd, Birmingham
and printed in Great Britain by
Redwood Burn Ltd, Trowbridge and Esher
for David & Charles (Publishers) Limited
Brunel House Newton Abbot Devon

Published in the United States of America
by David & Charles Inc
North Pomfret Vermont 05053 USA

CONTENTS

(*Title page*) Swan Green, Lyndhurst, Hampshire (*Patrick Eager*)

FOREWORD

Once, to speak of village cricket would have been tautological, for originally it was simply a village game. In the villages and on the open downland, the children's play grew into a men's game. The first great club, in the Meon valley village of Hambledon, laid down the enduring principles of the straight bat, length bowling and faithful fielding.

For some two centuries the game showed no essential change. The third stump was added; first, round-arm and then over-arm bowling was permitted; but the character of the game, like the character of the English village, remained the same. So that John Nyren in *The Cricketers of My Time*, Miss Mitford in *Our Village* and Hugh de Sélincourt in *The Cricket Match* were writing about the same subject over almost two hundred years.

Indeed, in north Hampshire in the 1930s there were two round-arm bowlers whose methods were the same as those of the men of the 1830s: and year in, year out, on all kinds of pitches, they were as successful as any others bowling there.

But change there was. Conscription in the First World War disturbed country life as nothing had done before. Young men whose ancestors as far back as memory ran had never been more than a dozen miles from their village found themselves deployed across Europe, Africa and Asia. A village could never be all the world again. Many came back to settle but the new-fangled motor cycle gave their sons the escape route to employment and entertainment in the nearby towns. As they went, and as farming was mechanised, the traditional country families increasingly left the countryside. In their places came retired people or commuters who wanted to live in villages, who took over the former labourers' cottages and made then look smarter than they had ever done.

Gerald Howat in this book has faced a task no one has undertaken before: to examine the phase of change in village cricket in tune with these changes in village life. He accepts that no one who has ever played village cricket has regarded it as anything but serious. A. G. Macdonnell, charming man and delightful humorist as he was, completely misunderstood the village game when he sent it up with his account of the bibulous 'literary gents' from London staging a match in the country in his *England, Their England*. It is still a serious matter, though perhaps not so grim as modern methods of preparing pitches replace the scythe, shears, grazing cattle and hand-mower of village days within living memory.

Now the man who takes guard to the first ball of a village match may well be a computer operator; the bowler a stockbroker; the wicket-keeper an electrician—all originating in distant parts of the country and choosing to live in this village. The batsman at the other end might even be an Australian. Only the first change bowler, hurrying up the road, is a 'local'—the publican.

Gerald Howat's fascinating book shows the continuation of the true strain of village cricket. Whether or not that strain survives, only the next few years will show. But he has crucially recognised, faced and relished examining the problem.

JOHN ARLOTT

PREFACE

Writing this book gave me the opportunity to visit village clubs throughout the British Isles. My route took me northwards to Yorkshire and across the border to the edge of the Scottish Highlands, and then south-westwards to the tip of Cornwall. Nearer at hand were the counties of the south-east where the game has its origins.

When winter came I turned to the treasured scrapbooks and anecdotal letters which people had sent me; to club Minutes and local histories; to old men's memories and faded photographs. I delved into the Bodleian Library, Oxford, and the newspaper section of the British Museum in London.

Village cricket, like so much else in our society, has changed a great deal during the thirty years in which I have played it. It is more proficient, more expensive and less picturesque than it once was. You will no more see a blacksmith in braces on the village green than a frockcoat and top hat at the Oval.

But so long as the game stays enjoyable, and there remain dedicated enthusiasts to cut wickets and sandwiches, it will survive—so long as the village itself survives. But that is another story.

Over 2,000 villages play cricket in these islands. I have not attempted a gazetteer of them all but I hope every village cricketer will recognise something of himself and of his own club, even if the names are different!

I have dedicated this book to my wife but I would also associate it with the many village cricketers with whom I have played, more especially those of Moreton Cricket Club where I have spent so many happy hours over the last twenty summers.

I would also thank John Arlott for agreeing to write a foreword and for his advice on the chapter on Hambledon.

GERALD HOWAT
North Moreton, Oxfordshire, 1980

1
THE CHANGING SCENE: THE BEGINNINGS TO 1914

'Park beside the Warner stand, gentlemen,' said the MCC attendant as a fleet of cars passed through the Grace Gates at Lord's. The cricketers made their way to the dressing-rooms on the first floor of the large, imposing, late-Victorian pavilion. The Mound Stand was filling up and already thirsty spectators had found their way to the new Tavern bar.

Presently, the fielding side walked through the Long Room passing the portrait of Sir Horatio Mann. On a wicket quicker than most in a wet summer, Tony Gauna, a left-arm seamer, broke through in the third over and conceded only sixteen runs in a lengthy opening spell. Gradually, a mastery was established and sustained all day.

Next morning, the *Daily Telegraph* cricket correspondent told his readers that: 'a magnificent unbeaten 51 by Nigel Thirkell, their leading all-rounder, gave the Kent side a four-wicket victory.'

One enthusiast turned to another: 'See Kent's won something else this year. Never heard of Gauna or Thirkell.' 'Not surprising really, it's not the Kent County side you know,' was the reply. 'It's a team from Linton Park, a village side in the county.'

'Famous village side,' he added. 'They've played cricket at Linton Park for over two hundred years. Sir Horatio Mann founded their club. And Thirkell's family go back a bit, too. His great-grandfather played for them in the old days of single-wicket games for high stakes.'

The village cricketers had, indeed, come to Lord's. Linton Park, in beating Toft from Cheshire, had become national champions. They came from a county where the game had been cradled. 'At the sport of cricket, of all the people in England, the Kentish folk are most renowned,' an eighteenth-century Earl of Oxford had noted. His fellow noblemen and landowners, men like John Sackville, third Duke of Dorset and Sir Horatio Mann, encouraged the game on their estates. They had wealth, the business acumen and the leisure to stage matches on which substantial bets were laid. The teams which they promoted would sometimes bear their own name and sometimes that of the village in which they owned land. They would entice players to join them with the offer of work on the estates.

(*left*) Sir Horatio Mann (*MCC*); (*right*) The Duke of Dorset (*MCC*)

Such a player was Valentine Romney who was given work as a gardener on the Dorset estate at Knole near Sevenoaks. He was possibly a good gardener since James Love, the poet, wrote of him:

> *Well-skill'd to spread the thriving plant around,*
> *And paint with fragrant flowers th'enamelled ground.*

He was evidently an excellent cricketer, 'the best in the world' said his obituary notice in the *Kentish Gazette*. He had sprung from the village of Meopham which was so proud of him that they allocated a pension of 1s 6d a week from the overseers' accounts to support his widow. The village kept up its payments and when she died in 1770, seventeen years after her husband, they paid our 2s 0½d for flannel and worsted to bury her. She has claims to be the first cricket widow.

Romney's family ran the hostelry in Meopham, The Harrow, whose name they changed to Ye 11 Cricketers. Cricket in that village owed its rise not to noble patronage but to the interest of the landlord, no doubt encouraged by the brewers. Meopham cricket reports occasionally appeared in the *Kentish Gazette*, such as their defeat of Chatham against odds of two to one.

Another match against Chatham a little later ended rather differently. Richard Hayes, a farmer, wrote in his diary on 10 July 1778:

> Meopham Fair. Cricket with Chatham. Ye Club is many of them gone to sea. No wonder they was beat.

Those players were victims of the press-gang which 'recruited' men for the American War of Independence. The Vestry Accounts showed that £5 5s 0d (a huge sum) had been paid to keep John Buggs from being 'pressed'—but whether he was a cricketer or not remains unknown.

Village matches in Kent—or anywhere else in the south-east—were of social and economic significance. They were linked to fairs or other public meetings and they were associated with heavy betting. An advertisement in the *Maidstone Journal* for 27 May 1800 is typical:

> This is to give Notice
> That on Whit-Thursday, being the Fair-Day, there will be a MATCH OF CRICKET PLAYED on WEST PECKHAM sporting place, between the gentlemen of Meopham against the gentlemen of East Peckham, for a Guinea each Man.

In Essex, a match between St Nicholas' Colchester, and Manningtree was played 'for eleven velvet caps', and one in Witney, Oxfordshire—between married men and bachelors—was 'for a considerable sum'. Many examples exist of such games, and, where money was involved, feelings could run high, as in the match between Great Sampford and Saffron Walden in 1794. The *Chelmsford Chronicle* reported that:

> Sampford finding themselves so completely beaten have refused to play the return match although Saffron Walden gave them the liberty, to make the match more equal, to take any man out of the Booking club or any adjoining parish. It is believed that Great Sampford will, for the future, be cautious who they challenge to play with.

The social side of these games made good business for local tradesmen. Fairs had been traditional holiday occasions for centuries. Racing was another feature linked to cricket. The cricketers of Great Bentley, in Essex, were invited in June 1785 to 'a match of cricket in the morning', followed by racing and then dinner 'at the Lion'.

Cricket came to take the place of the cruder sports of the eighteenth century. One Yorkshire parish paid men to play the game on Shrove Tuesday (how early in the season!), 'to entertain the populace and to prevent the infamous practice of throwing at cocks'. Various influences, such as the movement towards humanitarianism and the rise of Methodism, were making 'brutal' sports such as cock-fighting, bull-baiting, badger-baiting and pugilism unattractive. Cricket was a 'respectable' sport, as the *Public Advertiser* implied:

Eighteenth-century village cricket from the MCC collection of paintings (*MCC*)

> In the country, the ploughman, labourer and the artificer are satisfied with their holidays at Easter, Whitsuntide and Christmas. At the two former, they enjoy their innocent sports such as a cricket match or a game of cudgels or some other laudable trial of strength.

The 'respectable' sport became increasingly fashionable and clubs grew up all over the country in the immediate post-war period after the defeat of Napoleon in 1815. Football had not become a serious challenge and the Industrial Revolution had not yet caused a major movement to the towns. Gradually the patronage of aristocrats such as Dorset and Mann gave way to the paternalism of the village squire and parson.

The village game found its new patrons but did not necessarily lose its old ones. The earls of Darnley have been closely associated with another Kent side, Cobham, ever since the club's foundation in 1850. The club's *History* was written in 1899 by T. H. Baker; fewer than half-a-dozen copies survive of a slim green volume in which the author begins by saying that the club fulfilled 'the one great object of cricket, viz.—the bringing of all classes and ranks together in one common amusement.' Cobham, long before the official formation of the club, 'was always a cricketing village' as Richard Hayes' diary testified. In the 1770s he had watched Cobham play Addington and get 'rather ye worst of it'. Of another match, he 'left them at play, as it was not worth seeing'.

The Cobham of Baker's *History* was still a small village, often taking on local towns such as Gravesend and Rochester. It was essentially a local club, drawing on those born in the parish or living or working in it, though its links with the family of the earls of Darnley meant that guests staying at Cobham Hall were the 'occasional exception' to this. An annual fixture between the Hall and the Village took place on sixty-two occasions in the years covered by Baker's book, with the satisfying result of thirty wins to each side, a draw and a tie. For four seasons in the 1860s, the village season would end with a 'domestic match between two sides styled Federals and Confederates, apropos of the American Civil War then raging.'

The village team supplied 'seven more or less regular members' of the Kent XI, the most distinguished of whom was the Hon. Ivo Bligh who captained England in Australia in the 1882-3 series. He brought home from Australia a Melbourne girl as his wife, so that his performance in scoring 143 for Cobham single men v. married men not long before the tour could not be repeated for the same eleven!

Baker attributed Cobham's success 'to many causes, good captaincy, good batting and extraordinarily effective slow bowling', but most of all to fielding. 'Dropped catches were rare, and if a man had the ill-luck to make a miss, it was a long time before he heard the last of it.'

Bligh, in due course, became the eighth Earl of Darnley and the present earl is patron of the Club; its fixture list, taking 1979 as an example, retains a delightful

The Meopham side in 1893. Charlie Coombes is sitting on the ground on the left; the vicar, in a straw hat, is next to the captain

The Meopham side in 1912. Charlie Coombes is sitting on the extreme left; Robert Arnold is captain —with 27 playing years left

village flavour about it—Luddesdowne, Longfield Hill, Woodlands, Horton Kirby, Harvel and Minister.

One of the Cobham cricketers of the early 1890s was Robert Arnold, a young solicitor living in the village who had made the highest score of any Cobham player—163 for the Hall against the Village. Playing for Cobham against Meopham, he met the daughter of the Meopham president. Their marriage brought him to live in Meopham Court and to become the squire of the village.

The club had fallen on sad days because of the agricultural depression and because of the decline of self-employed craftsmen and tradesmen who could find the leisure to play. That the side recovered was due, initially, to Charlie Coombes, who scored five centuries in the 1890s. In the long run, both the club and the village owed a great deal to Arnold as cricketer, squire, solicitor and churchwarden. He was generous, and the teas served by maids from Meopham Court were lavish affairs for special matches. But he was also autocratic, especially in cricket matters, in a way which grew less acceptable to a later generation.

He was a man for whom 1914, the ending point of this chapter, was an artificial division in his career. He was still running the club along the same lines in the 1920s and 1930s. He became captain in 1898, thirty years later he shared in a last-wicket stand of 89 ensuring that his partner (at number ten) reached a century. After Meopham had made 248 and their opponents 335 there was still time for Meopham to bat again and reach 121 for seven. Arnold took the game seriously to the end of his life and disapproved of 'beer' matches. He was still playing in 1939!

Arnold may be taken as the typical squirearchal figure. As significant was the role of the parson in the nineteenth century. Parsons abound in the folklore of village cricket. There were 695 Oxford and Cambridge 'Blues' in the sixty-year reign of Queen Victoria. Two hundred and nine of them became Anglican clergymen and most of them found their way, at some time in their career, into a country living. But, first of all, we should notice the Reverend John Mitford, who was a parson in the eighteenth-century tradition, 'no more fit to be one than I am to be the Angel Gabriel,' as a friend remarked. Mitford had a number of parishes in Suffolk and was a man of many interests—gardening and writing among them—but his great passion was cricket. What cricket enthusiast cannot recognise something of himself in this letter of Mitford's?

> I lose all method, industry, fidelity and all other virtues, small and great, so long as summer lasts. I live out of doors like a wild man, never at home. Today cricket at Woodbridge, tomorrow at Ipswich, I play at Bury on Monday.

His friend corroborates the evidence:

> Mitford is gone crazy about cricket—he has, I am told, organised a cricket club in his parish, and enters into its advancement and success with all the interest of an amateur.

The Benhall Club sent a challenge the other day to the Saxmundham Club—and the approaching contest was a matter of as much discussion in the vicinity as the Battle of Waterloo was some few years bygone among politicians. The Benhallites were beaten and Mitford, so far as I hear, has kept house ever since. I fancy he has had a knock or two with the balls, for his letter talks of a disjointed thumb, a contusion on the hip, and a sightless eye. In another letter he described himself as bandaged from head to foot, and as full of sores as Lazarus.

The letter ended: 'Poor Mitford—I am sorry for his case: 'tis lucky we have an Asylum in the area.'

Mitford had introduced cricket to his parish in the 1820s. The Victorian parsons had one central reason for following his example—quite apart from their enjoyment of the game. Cricket was the way in which they might exercise paternal control over their flock. Paternalism meant several things: a straightforward fatherly concern; a way of bringing social groups together; and a desire to encourage temperate habits.

The Reverend James Pycroft, who played in the third University Match in 1836, and wrote one of cricket's most famous books, *The Cricket Field*, put something of these sentiments into the words of the (fictional) Reverend Henry Austin, in his semi-autobiographical novel *Elkerton Rectory*:

My cricket club was designed to encourage sympathy between man and man, however wide their ranks might be asunder, and most admirably did it conduce towards this end. The first thing was to lay down certain rules of conduct. All bad words and oaths—unhappily most of the idiom of the parish—should involve a forfeit or absence from the cricket field. Will Harris, a young miller, was a very fine, active man and a general favourite in Elkerton; so I made him my lieutenant in command and taught him to bowl in the fast underhand fashion. Young Jacques, Ben Cane and John Millwood, among others, quite caught the cricket mania, and the good result was that instead of vying with each other in smoking and drinking, and instead of lying about in bad company, these men were subjected to the improving influence of their Rector. By the end of the summer, eleven of Elkerton played eleven of Bourdon. But by the end of October, all cricket was at an end, and the public house was regaining its old customers. Idle habits threatened once more to prevail throughout the winter, and all this was the more to be regretted. So once more I set my wits to work to create a diversion in another way.

Charles Kingsley, author of *The Water Babies*, had the same outlook. In his own parish:

The young men used to take their bats and stumps to church and deposit them in the belfry till afternoon service was over, after which the adjournment to the field took place. They were dressed in their best with their sweethearts to look on. It was gala evening when the weather was warm and bright, and they were on their good behaviour, and I do not remember any riotous conduct or drunkenness arising out of it all.

This sort of sentiment was echoed by ordinary country parsons up and down the land. 'I established cricket,' wrote the Vicar of Camber in Kent in 1866, 'not so much for my own amusement but because it improved the morals of the labouring classes and often kept them from places where they could come to harm.' Cricket, in the small Dorset village of Bloxworth, was centred round the rectory where the Reverend Octavius Pickard-Cambridge, whose knowledge of spiders made him one of the leading arachnologists of the nineteenth century, taught his own sons to play the game. As the boys grew up, they coached the villagers and created a team that became one of the strongest village sides in the county. Pickard-Cambridge liked the day of a village match and he would be found busy putting up tents and encouraging everyone to come and watch. Like so many Victorian parsons, he was an 'all-rounder' in a wider sense than as a cricketer. Besides spiders, music was an important interest in his life, as was church architecture. But the villagers thought that what he did for their cricket was the most important contribution!

Some clergy may have pushed their associations with the game a bit far. One Welsh village incumbent in the 1870s required the players, before every match, to 'attend morning service in cricket costume'. Others, such as the Vicar of Chipstead in Wiltshire, simply offered the facilities—the church vestry as a pavilion and the hymn-board placed outside as a scoreboard.

Finally, there were the henpecked ones! When the Vicar of Earlswood in Warwickshire got married, his wife forbade the club to use his gaunt Victorian vicarage as a club-house any more.

The Anglican clergy, on the whole, did not mind Sunday cricket. One archdeacon announced that he found it beneficial to stage a village match between Sunday morning and evening service. It brought down upon him the wrath of a Presbyterian minister, the Reverend Dr Hugh Howat, who wrote:

> The advocacy of Sunday cricket clubs by an archdeacon—does any man in his senses doubt that the handwriting on the wall has gone out against the Church of England already? The shepherds, in place of leading their flocks to green pastures, are leading them only to the barren heath, the sinking morass and the river of death.

Since the minister was the author's great-grandfather, let the matter rest there!

The squires and parsons represented one strand in the evolution of village cricket after the decline of aristocratic influence. But the game drew strength from other quarters, notably through the development of the mining communities in the Industrial Revolution. One such community was the Nottinghamshire village of Annesley, through which parish thousands pass daily as they drive up and down the M1. Long before arterial roads and motorways were thought of, Robertus Hode (the Robin Hood of legend and ballad), dwelt there. Centuries passed and in the dawn of the industrial age, the poet Byron came and found inspiration. Soon the

Annesley in 1860; an extremely old photograph—many of the players have moved their heads during the long exposure

hills and tufted shades of which he wrote were scarred by mines. Shafts were sunk and cottages built. A small community of managers, officials and miners were bound by a common purpose and by shared dangers. As some compensation for the ardours of life, the colliery company started a cricket club. The men of Annesley village played their cricket in the 1860s and onwards on the ground by the Park. The children played well into the night by the light of street gas-lamps—as described by another of Annesley's sons, D. H. Lawrence.

Competitive colliery cricket was almost as demanding as the daily lives of those who played it. From this stern stable of Annesley came one more famous name. Harold Larwood left the mines behind him for ever to become one of the fastest bowlers of his day and to rout the 1932-3 Australians. Cricket in the mining villages of the North and Midlands has made its own contribution to the long line of men, especially fast bowlers, who have played cricket for England.

Not far from Annesley is another colliery village, that of Cresswell on the Derbyshire-Nottinghamshire border where the Slater family made their contribution to village cricket. The senior cricketing member of the family, Harry, had taken part in a Midlands travelling cricketing circus: 'The clown cricketers would provide burlesque entertainment often mimicking the game they then played in earnest.' They were much in demand at fêtes and galas. Harry's sons included Herbert (who was good enough to play occasionally for Derbyshire but who declared his preference for the village side), Harry, Arthur, Sam and Archie. Archie, on his debut for Cresswell in 1909, was top-scorer with 5 out of 9. Later he played for Derbyshire, and for Bacup and for Colne in the great days of the Lancashire League in the 1930s. The Slater family—Harry's sons and grandsons—took on their own village of Cresswell and, as a team, would play against other colliery village sides.

Harry, junior, wrote to me:

> I have been looking back over my records of cricket seventy years ago. Travel for away matches was by horse-drawn waggonette. The players took sandwiches with them. The wickets were good unless rain interfered during the match. The match of all the Slaters against Cresswell was the largest gate of spectators in the history of Cresswell Cricket Club. Now mines around this area have been worked out and cricket around our locality is not as it used to be.

Another family side of the period was that of the Colmans, who played their cricket against villages in Norfolk in the 1840s. Robert and Ann Colman had fifteen children, three of whom, James, Jeremiah and Edward, set up a business to market the mustard which the family farm milled. Records in the *Norfolk News* report some of the matches in which the eleven brothers participated. All their games had this in common: the cricketers afterwards 'sat down to a sumptuous dinner'. Roast beef with mustard, no doubt!

Yet another cricketing family were the Thewlis who played for the Yorkshire village side of Lascelles Hall. Three of them often played for Yorkshire itself and the whole family produced an eleven in 1866 which played Chickenley, and won. Even the umpire, scorer and man on the gate were Thewlis!

But no family could outdo the achievements of the Robinsons who fielded a side against various West Country villages from 1878 till 1964, principally playing the Somerset village of Flax Bourton on the August bank-holiday weekend. Over one hundred Robinsons have turned out for the team. A few played first-class cricket and one of them, Douglas, a Gloucestershire player for many years, was selected to play for the Gentlemen against the Players in 1914.

One day in August 1891 the Robinson family accepted a challenge from the Grace family. It was, of course, scarcely village cricket, but it deserves to be noticed since both families made so big a contribution to village cricket near Bristol. The Graces turned out in full strength. W.G. captained the side which included his brothers E.M. and G.F. The Grace family made 184 of which E.M. made 81 and W.G. 12. Crescens Robinson replied with 67 but the last eight wickets fell for 42, and the Robinsons lost by 37 runs.

The Robinson family team which played Flax Bourton in 1883; Crescens is sitting with a bat

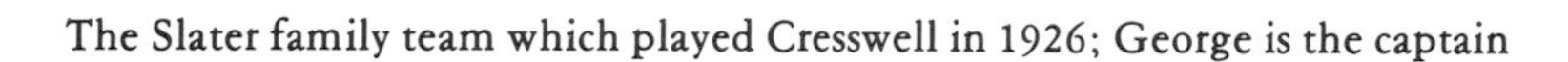

The Slater family team which played Cresswell in 1926; George is the captain

This was the most important game the Robinsons ever played. They continued to field an eleven until 1964. A family tree of them shows five generations of cricketers in the direct line and a family statistician has compiled a magnificent table of averages in which seven men scored over one thousand runs, nineteen scored centuries, and seven led the team over its eighty-six years of life. Of them, the writer Bernard Darwin remarked: 'so brave a family team as this, which has gone on for so long with recurrent reinforcements, seems to me to afford interesting material for the eugenists. They draw up their pedigrees of the Bachs in music and, if a family black sheep may say so, the Darwins in science.'

The family eleven may no longer play but 210 Robinsons assembled at Flax Bourton in August 1978 to celebrate the centenary of the fixture against the village. To the Grace family and village cricket, we shall return in Chapter 5.

Probably half the village clubs of today were founded at some time in the nineteenth century, owing their origins to the growth of industrial communities or the paternalism of particular individuals. The land on which Gosforth in Northumberland played had once belonged to Job Bulman who made his money in the East India Company in the eighteenth century. For a single season, the cricket club founded there played as Bulman's village. The match billed in a poster in late September 1865 was possibly its last as Bulman's village. For the first sixteen years of its life, the club gave the ball (in home matches) to the top scorer until it found this too expensive!

Several clubs can claim to have been founded because of the arrival of the railway—or rather, because of the men building it. Navvies working on the Chester-Holyhead railway in the 1850s, for example, helped to establish the game in Wales where one contemporary remarked that it was pleasing to 'notice the ruddy glow imparted to the countenances of the navvies by this delightful pastime.'

Among other examples are the clubs at Seaton Carew in Durham and Blackheath in Surrey. Seaton Carew was founded in 1829 by prosperous Quaker families who left Darlington to spend the summer in their country houses in the village, while Blackheath's club was founded in the 1870s because of the growth of a local gunpowder industry. Farningham in Kent, on the other hand, owed little to local interest and in its early days drew upon players coming down from London in their traps and four-in-hands.

The village cricketers of the nineteenth century played their games in a rural setting which remained substantially unchanged up to the outbreak of the First World War. None the less, the game suffered in the second half of that century from the agricultural depression when wages fell and unemployment was rife. There was a steady movement to the towns, village communities shrank and numbers declined. Furthermore, increased mobility led to some 'poaching' of players of ability to nearby town clubs. Those who stayed in the village often

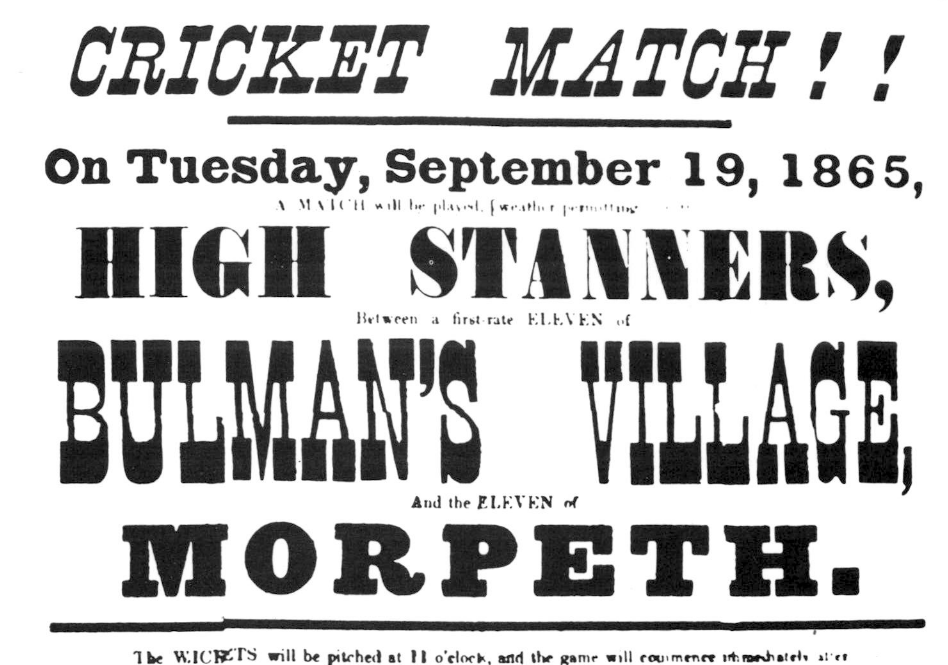

Publicity for the match! (*Museum of English Rural Life*)

worked long hours in the fields and found it difficult to find the time for cricket. Some village sides collapsed through lack of support.

What was the game like for those village players of the pre-1914 era? Numbers aside, their problems were the eternal ones of village cricket: ground, transport, food and finance.

It is difficult for us to realise how important the horse was to those cricketers. The groundsman whose club owned its own horse would have to muck out the stables, feed and water the animal and put on its leather boots before beginning work on the outfield. It explains an entry in the accounts of Earlswood: '1879, £1 1s 0d to the saddler for boots' (for the horse!). Clubs in the mining areas would often borrow a coal-haulier's horse and return it in time for delivering coal in winter. One club recorded ruefully: 'Our horse wouldn't wear leather boots,' while another sought guidance on how to give an injured horse a poultice.

Wickets were cut by a scythe and the outfield would be lucky if it saw anything more than a few sheep in the season. One club experimented with a mallet to flatten its wicket. While many pitches must have been rough, it was by no means the story everywhere. The club in North Wales who protested to their opponents in 1859 clearly expected something better: 'the ground was extremely bumpy, the creases not marked out, there was no table for the scorers, no tent, and worst of all, no refreshments.' The report added: 'The remarks were made in no unkind spirit because it is indispensable to render a cricket match what it should be.' A comment with which all cricketers would entirely agree. We like things to be ship-shape and admire a club which presents an image of good organisation and devoted care.

It would be unfair to those who gave such devoted care if one did not recognise the unsung groundsmen who did their best. The ground in Lascelles Hall was lovingly cared for, sown with lawn seed and white clover, and so well tended that its curator, John Lockwood, was soon called to serve at the Oval. For many years before 1914 (and as many after), Willie Scott, the groundsman at St Boswells in Roxburghshire, cycled six miles each way to care for the pitch. Against odds, many such Willie Scotts laboured south of the border as well.

The effect of poor wickets was twofold: scores were low and injuries were high. Low scores were the rule rather than the exception, and explain why matches were so frequently two innings apiece. When leisure was limited good cricketing time could not be wasted, and the second innings was taken just as seriously as the first.

How did those cricketers get to their matches, or even know they were going to take place? Newspapers and handbills were a common way in the eighteenth century of announcing sides, venue and places for teams to assemble. The more common device through much of the pre-1914 period was the simple one of telling players week-by-week and, in small communities, knocking on the doors of late replacements. One martinet of a captain required fifteen men to be ready and changed before he would inform four of them to stand down for the day. Fixtures were not arranged with the efficiency of modern club secretaries. In some cases the vicar would arrange them, and, no doubt, regular winter meetings with his fellow clergy in the rural deanery achieved much in that direction.

Players would be likely to travel by horse-brake, pony-trap or farm waggon. One club hired the local hearse on the principle that no one wanted to be buried on Saturday. At Holbeck in Yorkshire they chartered a corn-waggon. The poorer members of the Wirksworth side in Derbyshire went by horse-brake and the richer ones in their own carriages—an imposing cavalcade calculated to put the opposition into disarray! The cricketers from Bures in Essex had a well-planned route which allowed the horses to drink at the Doctor's Pond and themselves at the Red Lion, on their way to Great Bentley. Our ancestors were hardy travellers: the cricketers of Seaton Carew made an eighty-mile round trip on the roughest of

Refreshments after the match at Lydney in Gloucestershire in 1885

roads by pony-trap to play Whitby in the 1850s. Many Yorkshire villages such as these used sailing vessels to make their way along the North Sea coast to play each other. As the cricketers of one Yorkshire village side disappeared into the gathering gloom, the last their hosts heard 'was a parting solo on the horn across the waters'.

From 1840 onwards a network of railways sprang up throughout the country. There is some evidence of their use by village cricketers and they became the means by which larger clubs established north-south cricket links in the nineteenth century. One Yorkshire village team's day began and ended with a four-hour train journey—home by 3 a.m.!

Later, the bicycle offered more prospects. The Blackheath cricketers found they could tie pads and bat to the crossbar and make their way in convoy. Many a village cricketer blessed an invention which, in its own way, created a major social revolution in Edwardian times.

Feeding habits underwent considerable change in the eighteenth and nineteenth centuries. Village cricket in the earlier period was linked, as we have seen, to fairs and other activities. Landlords reckoned to do well out of these occasions and would advertise an 'ordinary', which was a lunch, for both players and spectators. 'The Cricketers Arms' became a popular name associating club and pub.

Gradually, the 'ordinary' disappeared with the end of the betting era. As the game settled down into its nineteenth-century pattern—essentially one of small village units—it became the custom to eat after the game was over. Many a small club settled for bread and cheese and onions to eat and ale to drink. Others might have a cold meat tea in the village hall. The press coverage of a match in Kent in 1867 is almost entirely devoted to what was eaten and drunk with the comment: 'in regard to the play itself, but little need be mentioned.' For two major games in 1882, Lascelles Hall stocked up with half a gallon of whisky, a gallon of brandy, half a gallon of rum, nine boxes of ginger-beer, thirty lbs of beef, two hams and twelve dozen pies! Tea in the middle of the game was most unusual in village cricket in the period before 1914.

Financial affairs are chiefly of interest for their evidence of how little things once cost! Bridlington in Yorkshire financed their first season for £6 13s 9d including the purchase of a bench for spectators. To pay about 12s 6d for a bat was as fair a price in 1880 as in 1850. Farningham were paying 6s a ball in 1859, and also finding 10s a match for their umpire—a most generous fee.

Batting gloves in the mid-century cost 8s, wicket-keeping gloves 10s, and a score book 7s. Among the more unusual entries, compared with modern needs, were those paying a man to drive the trap, or buying horses' shoes or boots. These are figures which take on some meaning when set against wage-patterns and the cost of living. An agricultural worker earned from 7s 6d to 13s 6d between 1850 and 1900. His beer was 2d a pint and tobacco 2d an ounce. A large loaf of bread cost 8d and coal was 1s a hundredweight.

Fund-raising played little part in village activities. The benevolent patron (later dignified with the title 'vice-president') was expected to contribute between 5s and £1. Among the more unusual ways of raising money was a soirée such as that held by Earlswood, and a concert at St Boswells in which the principal soprano was secured from the Carl Rosa Opera Company. Wirksworth saved themselves a lot of trouble by appointing a 'collector of subscriptions' who got 5 per cent commission.

Unique must be the comment of Hawick's historian who recorded: 'Notwithstanding the generous treatment by successive dukes, we have always had a struggle to make ends meet.' The canny Scot might almost be believed were it not for the evidence of his own club's fund-raising. Hawick held a club bazaar in 1899 which raised £750. The figure, in modern terms, must represent several thousands. The purist may argue that Hawick is (or was) scarcely a village. Maybe! But the club has always played its cricket on the Scottish border village circuit.

The discipline imposed on village cricketers seems strange to us—after all, they were supposed to be playing for fun. If you were late at Lascelles Hall you paid fines—to be spent 'in the pub the night they are inflicted'. Another Yorkshire club, Helmfirth, forbade its players 'to smoke or lie on the ground during play'.

At Groombridge in Kent you were suspended for seven days if you entered the

EARLSWOOD

CRICKET CLUB.

THE ANNUAL

SOIREE

WILL TAKE PLACE ON

MONDAY, DECEMBER 26th, 1904,

IN THE

SCHOOL ROOM, SALTER STREET,

On behalf of the Funds of the above Club.

COMMITTEE:

Rev. G. W. Barnard, Messrs. J. Osborne, T. A. Meakes, F. Hunt, S. Hunt, F. G. Burgoyne, H. Wyatt, T. W. Holtom, and E. Hunt.

M.C's - Messrs. H. J. Summers and E. Hunt.

DANCING TO COMMENCE AT 8 p.m. Carriages at 3 a.m.

TICKETS 1/6 EACH.

AN EFFICIENT QUADRILLE BAND WILL BE IN ATTENDANCE.

S. SMITH, PRINTER & STATIONER (Opposite Church) HENLEY-IN-ARDEN.

A pleasant way to spend Boxing Day evening and raise money for the club ground 'otherwise than by the gate'. Groombridge, as a club, stood no nonsense. They refused to renew the fixture against Cowden in 1911 because of press comments on Groombridge's umpire in Cowden's report!

A century earlier, a report in the *York Herald* of September 1814 also concerned the umpires:

> The Yarn players were extremely sorry that they had not a favourable opportunity of returning thanks to the umpires who had had to go some distance after the game and had their carriages waiting in the lane.

Umpires, at that time, were gradually ceasing to play another role—that of manager. In the days of heavy betting a side's umpire would sometimes manage a side and give advice on whether or not a match should be conceded.

It is difficult to generalise on what village cricketers wore in this period. To play in the ordinary working-clothes of the day became less acceptable as the game advanced. Clubs with aristocratic patronage sported their lord's colours by wearing distinctive hats and coats. *The Liverpool Mercury* of October 1811 put it into verse:

> *White hats of scarce four ounces;*
> *A jacket smart, flesh-coloured hose;*
> *a cricketer complete compose.*

Breeches were giving way to trousers which that famous village cricketer, the Reverend John Mitford deplored, since they 'got in the way of the ball'. Coloured shirts, sometimes with a neck-tie, were favoured, while waistcoats did service as sweaters and bowler hats as head-gear. One club's Minute of 1858 offers a curious tail-piece on dress: 'Approved that the secretary order at least one buttonhook for the use of such members as may be inclined to walk home with their boots buttoned.' By the 1880s the more prosperous village cricketers were sporting blazers with buttons to the top and matching caps. Indeed, photographs of village sides between 1860 and 1914 have an interest of their own in their portrayal of social distinctions within the community.

We have got our players to their matches, financed them, and fed them. How did they fare in the games themselves? The scores of countless village cricket matches played in the two centuries before 1914 lie in the archives of newspapers, in treasured scrapbooks and in a very few surviving beautifully written score-books. Such score-sheets, especially if accompanied by a newspaper account in which adjectives like 'unexampled', . 'capital' and 'worthy' abound, are evocative documents. The *Ipswich Journal* of 27 July 1844 describes

> . . . an unexampled feat at cricket. At a match of cricket last week between Boxted and Great Bentley, Mr John Almond Junior, one of the bowlers, had the good fortune to put

Two Oxfordshire sides at the turn of the century: Horspath posing for a team photograph and Garsington setting off for an away match (*Museum of English Rural Life*)

out the whole side of the Boxted gentlemen by his own hand, in the following manner, viz., by bowling down seven wickets, two catches and stumping one. This feat, is, we believe, unparalleled in the annals of cricket.

It was the day of the four-ball over, with the bowler keeping wicket at the other end, and bowlers getting credit only if they secured the wicket unaided.

Forty years later there was another 'unexampled feat' when the Essex village of Rickling Green played the Orleans Club in August 1882. Rickling Green were all out for 94 and their opponents passed their score for the loss of one wicket. In the fashion of the day, they went on batting and their second wicket pair added 507! After Mr Vernon had been dismissed for 250 and Mr Trevor for 338, Mr Spiro weighed in with a 50 and Mr Partridge took a further 90 off a tired attack. Rickling Green took some comfort from taking the last wicket just before stumps were drawn at 6.30. The Orleans' total of 920, as the *Essex Observer* reported, had now become the 'tallest innings on record' surpassing the 775 made by New South Wales against Victoria at Sydney six months earlier. The Rickling Green men had bowled 293 four-ball overs.

A total of nearly 700 had been made the year before by Thornbury in Gloucestershire but such events were very far from normal. For a genuine village side to total more than 100 was unusual right up until 1914. Innings were fast and furious, usually lacking much in the way of scientific batting, and followed breathlessly by a second innings—at least by one side.

The technique of bowling underwent more radical change than that of batting in the nineteenth century. Those who bowled before 1828 delivered an underarm ball which, in a really great bowler such as David Harris of Hambledon, could combine length, direction and pace with a quick 'lift' off the pitch. Gradually, many of these 'lob' bowlers began to raise their arm to the height of their shoulders. Despite criticism that such an action involved throwing, this 'round-arm' bowling was declared legal in 1828—provided no throw (or bending of the elbow) was involved. One of the arguments in favour of change had been that batsmen were dominating bowlers to an extent detrimental to the game. Yet, as village cricketers assimilated the change, batsmen prospered rather better—the bowlers found the new technique difficult.

A generation later saw the law changed again, in 1864, to legalise over-arm bowling. Just as changes in architectural style made their way slowly from the metropolis to rural communities, so the niceties of legislative innovation made their impact in a leisurely manner on the village cricketer.

Towards the end of the nineteenth century standards changed for clubs joining the newly-formed leagues. In the North of England and in the Midlands League cricket simply meant playing within a competition according to rules laid down by the organising committee of the league. League cricket permitted an element of

'Rural Sports or a Cricket Match Extraordinary', a watercolour by Rowlandson (*MCC*)

professionalism while fulfilling its main purpose of providing a structure within which the amateur could play.

While the more famous leagues generally attracted clubs and players of a level well above village standard, there were, nevertheless, village sides to be found in their ranks. Church and Enfield were founder-members of the Lancashire League in 1890; Pudsey St Lawrence belonged to the Bradford League; the Staffordshire League included the village of Ashcombe Park.

Other leagues, with less famous names, made a particular appeal to village clubs, as for example, the Saddleworth and District League for villages on the Lancashire and Cheshire borders; the Huddersfield and District League attracting Lascelles Hall, Almondbury and Linthwaite; and the Bassetlaw and District League welcoming villages, as much as towns' and works' teams, within the Derbyshire, Staffordshire, Nottinghamshire and Yorkshire areas, based on Chesterfield.

While league cricket before the First World War made little impact in the South of England, the activities in Cornwall provided an important exception; numerous villages entered the Cornish East or West League. But, overall, league cricket's dominance of the village game was to come much later in the twentieth century.

Village cricket has never been entirely monopolised by men. Women played the game in the eighteenth century and their cricket enjoyed some importance between 1745 and 1790. In the South-east, village sides were found in Westdean, Chilgrove, Charlton, Moulsey Hurst, Upham, Felley Green and Ganderston. Matches received some coverage in the press and could draw crowds of over a thousand.

The *London Magazine* advertised a game for 13 July 1747:

> This day, July 13, will be played in the Artillery Ground, the match of cricket so long expected, between the women of Charlton, in Sussex, against the women of Westdean, and Chilgrove, in the same county. It is hoped, that the paying sixpence of admission to this match will not be taken amiss, the charges thereof amounting to upwards of four score pounds. Wickets pitched at 2 o'clock.

On the following day, the same paper reported that:

> In playing the above match, the company broke in, so that it was impossible for the game to be played out; and some of them being very much frightened, and others hurt, it could not be finished till this morning (July 14) when at 9 o'clock they will start to finish the same, hoping the company will be so kind as to indulge them in not walking within the ring, which will not only be a great pleasure to them, but a general satisfaction to the whole. All ladies and gentlemen who have paid to see this match on Monday, shall have the liberty of the ground to see it finished, without any other charge. And in the afternoon they will play a second match in the same place, several large sums being depending. The women of the Hills of Sussex will be in orange-coloured ribbons, and those of the Dales in blue; wickets will be pitched at 1 o'clock, and begin at 2.

Clearly, betting made the games attractive to watch while small prizes, such as a barrel of ale, a cake, gloves or a piece of lace would be offered to players. To win was enough if your small village triumphed over a larger one, as did the ladies of Rotherby in Leicestershire in August 1792. Their defeat of Hoby led to their being 'placed in a sort of triumphant car, preceded by music and flying streamers and conducted home by the youth of Rotherby.' So reported the *Sporting Magazine*.

Even when the women were not playing, they might provide pre-match entertainment as the *London Morning Advertiser*, much earlier in the century, tells of a village game in Kent:

> The gentlemen who play this match have subscribed for a Holland smock of one guinea value, which will be run for by two jolly wenches, one known by the name of the Little Bit of Blue and the other, Black Bess. They are to run in drawers only and there is excellent sport expected. Captain Vigers with a great many of his bruisers and bull-dogs will attend to make a ring.

At the dawn of the Victorian age, women village cricketers had a last, belated 'fling' in a match at Sileby in Nottinghamshire in 1833. The *Nottingham Review* reported events with some sadness:

Two impressions of ladies playing village cricket in the nineteenth century; 'it gives an opportunity for the wearing of some very pretty costumes and it amuses the other sex' (*MCC and from* The Graphic *June 1890*)

Saturday, 1 August 1914: the cricketers of Corringham in Essex (*Museum of English Rural Life*)

> There were frequent applications to the tankard so that they rendered themselves objects such as no husbands, brothers, parents and lovers could contemplate with any degree of satisfaction.

Far more in keeping with the nineteenth century were the ladies of Walham whose match between maidens and matrons, in 1835, was followed by country dances and a supper. Victorian lady-cricketers, said *The Graphic*, were decorous, modest and (for the men) harmlessly amusing. If such condescension discouraged them from playing, at least they were welcome as supporters where 'a very liberal allowance of the fair sex' would support one men's club in the days before 1914.

So let us leave the village cricketer playing on a summer's day on Saturday 1 August 1914. It is bank-holiday weekend and the sun is shining fitfully. Half the side is in white flannels and the ladies are trying out the new-fangled idea of tea between the innings. The vicar is playing and so is the blacksmith. The squire's son has had to drop out because of a Territorial camp. Farmer Brown has spared some of his labourers from harvesting. The local photographer has been asked to come along and the picture he takes may have some nostalgic value for that village club. Let him get on with taking it, anyway, before the clouds roll up.

2
THE CHANGING SCENE: 1914 TO THE PRESENT DAY

Village cricket was one of the nation's institutions which suffered severely because of the First World War. The game simply stopped, and for a variety of reasons. Some thought it unpatriotic to play. As one club put it: 'there will be no further games until Kaiser Bill and his hordes are beaten.' Fields disappeared under the plough in the need for increased food production. Most of all, the cricketers left to go to war.

When they came back—some of them—they resumed their playing of a game which had changed far less than the world to which they had returned. Squirearchal figures such as Robert Arnold at Meopham still dominated the scene. Not until after the Second World War was their generous hospitality to be diminished by the claims of social egalitarianism and by taxation. As late as 1932 a young man of wealth could write to his mother of village cricket in Sussex:

> I played cricket for Shoreham. It is all very nice and patriarchal. People quite obviously like to see me there. Working men seem to weave a romantic halo about the gentry.

Vice-presidents still provided the larger share of the club's revenue and would be expected to donate anything up to £5—a sizeable sum when £400 was a professional man's salary. Even in 1963 one Berkshire village was required by its chairman to keep the players' subscription at 5s because 'we don't expect them to pay for their cricket'.

In many ways, the game retained its rustic features. The old England captain, A. E. R. Gilligan, found this when he watched some village matches on behalf of the *News Chronicle* in the 1930s. One particular visit which delighted him was to Grove in Berkshire. He watched them play Littleworth. Three Grove men were fined 2d each for making a duck. The Littleworth opening bat retired to hospital after long-leg's throw-in floored him. Most of all, the pavilion appealed to Gilligan. It was the horse box in which Humourist, winner of the 1921 Derby, had travelled to the course. Another club, even less well provided for, had a tree which fulfilled various roles during the afternoon: from its branches hung the score; under its spread players had tea; and behind its foliage they relieved themselves.

The village game changed little after the war; compare this Horspath side of 1924 with the earlier photograph on page 28 (*Museum of English Rural Life*)

Nor did the game cost very much. Great Dunmow in Essex spent modestly on some essential needs. Compare their figures for 1923 with those of 1979:

	1923			*1979*	*Multiple of increase*
	£	s	d	£p	
Fire insurance	0	2	6	9.93	× 79
Fixture cards	1	0	0	17.82	× 18
Bats (per bat)	1	10	0	18.00	× 12
Balls (per ball)	0	10	0	5.50	× 11
Score book	0	3	0	3.60	× 24

Another club's 1936 figures may be compared with its 1979 ones. In 1936 they received £31 of which £19 came from vice-presidents. They spent £9 on kit, £1 17s on hiring a roller, and bought a tent (which they still use) for £5 5s. In 1979 their income was £1,552 of which £313 went on a new spiking and raking machine and £159 on seed, loam and fertiliser.

The financial contrast, as we all know, is not so much between the 1890s and 1930s as between the 1930s and 1970s. One victim of inflation was the vice-

TUPPENCE A DUCK—
AND HEFTY SIXES

The pavilion—once a horse-box—and some spectators on the Grove, Berkshire, village cricket ground on Saturday.

The horse-box pavilion at Grove in Berkshire which Gilligan admired, as drawn by Cumberworth of the *News Chronicle*

president. 'Many of us are retired professional people. We have a great deal less money than the players,' one commented. A treasurer sadly (in more senses than one) ticked off the generals who had died in the past ten years. Rather more pertinently, the remark was made with some frequency, 'Let the players pay for their cricket, they play it.' At something between £5 and £10 for a subscription the players of 1979 paid. But the game was still cheap, compared with golf or riding to hounds. The annual dinner could cost more than the sub.

The fund-raising devices of earlier years continued between the wars—bazaars, whist drives, jumble sales and draws. But the 1970s produced more efficient money-raising events such as bingo and various pool schemes. Most of all, bar profits were a major source of income in clubs which took on the responsibility of having a liquor licence and gave up using the local pub.

Cricket teas, as we have seen, were only just coming into vogue before 1914. They have been an essential feature ever since. Between the wars, sixpence (or 2½p) was the normal price. In Barnby Dun in Yorkshire the opposition got tea (with food) for 3d: the home team were given a cup of tea for nothing.

Teas in general are the same the whole country over, with regional variations such as scones in Scotland, cold meat in the North and splits in the West Country. The immediate post-1945 period of austerity and rationing caused problems. One Essex club noted that as late as 1952 it catered for nine home matches with 1¾ lb of tea, 4½lb of margarine and 5 lb of sugar. With such iron rations (presumably true everywhere) the players of Butleigh in Somerset must have welcomed the gift of two flagons of home-made cider per match. And if you have ever tried to play cricket on home-made cider . . . Better, perhaps, to wait until the game is over and draw on the churchwarden clay pipes, by long tradition supplied to members at Ifield in Sussex.

Between the wars the charabanc appeared as a popular form of transport for taking players and their families for an away match. Farm lorries were used instead of horse-drawn vehicles. Bicycles were common and, surprisingly frequently, the branch lines of the old railway system. Many a village team found it simple and relatively cheap to take the local train two or three stations down the line. If you travelled by car you were someone of some standing in the community. It was the years after 1945 which brought players to the villages by car as a matter of course. The sight, in the 1970s, of village cricketers lining the green with their splendid models had something to do with the decline in vice-presidential donations! One club, pressed for time, actually took to the air.

With the outbreak of war in 1939 the cricketers, like everyone else, faced the second challenge within a generation. 'It was no part of Hitler's scheme that any able-bodied Briton of cricketing age should be left on this side of the Channel,' minuted Farningham. Farningham found their own ground in Kent used as headquarters for the barrage balloon defences. Airmen slept in the pavilion and built bunkers on the pitch itself. Lorries carrying cylinders of gas made the ground unrecognisable.

Kent, by its geographical position, was the county most affected by the war since it represented the front line of aerial defence against the invader. A farmer whose barn was destroyed by a doodlebug commented: 'Thank God it wasn't the square.' Cudham, with rare foresight, designed their mortuary and gas-cleansing station so that it could become a new pavilion when the war was over.

Unlike 1914, the war did not stop the game completely, either at club or village level. Servicemen were able to relax if they were lucky enough to be posted near a cricket ground, and this was particularly true for aircrews flying by night and living at some south-east coast base by day. Far from being closed by the war, the village cricket club at Chapelizod in County Dublin was founded in war-time. Of course, Eire was neutral but there was a Local Security Force—a sort of Home Guard. A ground was acquired near the river Liffey and these volunteer defenders prepared a wicket, bought some kit, painted their shoes white and found some old white flannels in the market. Richard Malone's mother made eleven caps, panelled in green and white. A dog was hired—and fed at 4s a season—to retrieve the ball from the Liffey.

Endeavour fostered success. Chapelizod reached the final of a Junior Village Cup competition. They dared not play George, the treasurer, the best club-man in the village but no performer. They hated to hurt his feelings. A handy solution arose in a 'friendly' game. George was doing duty umpiring at square leg while a fellow batsman was in. A full toss hit squarely to leg did just enough damage to George's shin to enable Chapelizod to win the cup. George was only a spectator but it was he who was fined drunk-in-charge after the celebrations.

When the war ended—against Germany in May 1945—many a village club got going the same summer. As one boasted, 'within weeks, nay days, of the defeat of Hitler, a team was in the field.' The change in village cricket was much more marked than it had been in 1919. Villages became less rural and their cricket became more technically proficient.

The rural community lost whatever isolation it had once retained as housing developments and estates grew up. Some villages became swallowed up as suburbs of towns. One elderly exile, in the 1970s, returned to the scene of his distant youth. He recalled the winding lanes and the silence of his childhood. Eventually, he stopped at a garage in a crowded shopping area and asked where the village was. 'You're in it, mate,' was the blunt reply.

Increased mobility meant that some villages became 'dormitories' for commuters. All this had its effect on cricket. The commuters would have to spend their weekends catching up on the gardening. Good village players might be seduced by town clubs and depart, driving past the very green itself, for a club with better standards and facilities. Family life made more demands in that the family man was expected to behave as such, and not play cricket all weekend. Clubs could no longer count on the dedicated loyalty of their players. By the 1960s a general depression had touched cricket. The game went into decline and some village sides collapsed altogether.

One club which ended its life at the end of the 1969 season was Staines Linoleum in Middlesex, founded in 1894 when the new inlaid lino was coming into fashion. A small industry grew up in a rural part of Staines. The first Minutes

A Haig match in progress at Collingham; whisky, of course, is advertised and the home side wins

of the club record the securing of a place to play on the 'Moor between Hammond's Farm and the London and South-West Railway' and the purchase of caps at 1s 11½d each. One of the those caps went to young Joe Caiger, whose association with Staines Lino cricket lasted throughout the club's history, so that he was present, as an old man of ninety-one, at the final match—surely a unique achievement!

Cricket, at all levels, was given a new lease of life by the beginnings of commercial sponsorship. Competitions such as the Gillette, John Player and Benson and Hedges, gave the first-class game the fillip it needed. Lively television presentation made the game attractive to new audiences. By 1972 sponsorship had reached village cricket, and its arrival helped (together with the growth of league cricket) to bring back the game's popularity.

The firm of John Haig & Co Ltd, in conjunction with *The Cricketer* magazine, launched a knock-out competition for village clubs which attracted an entry of over 800 clubs. It was the biggest competition in the game and involved considerable organisation. Every fortnight throughout the summer a round was completed and secretaries had to send in their 'returns' in time for the administrative arrangements for the next round to be made, an enterprise run from *The Cricketer* office.

The competition gave village cricketers prizes in cash and kind for achievements at various stages. Shields, ties and whisky were on offer, just for entering, in the 'honeymoon' period of the competition. New clubs were introduced to each other and successful ones crossed county borders to meet their opponents. County and regional champions emerged. The ultimate goal was the final at Lord's itself. If there were reservations, they came from the secretaries of successful clubs who found their traditional fixture lists upset every other Sunday. One solution was a quick pairing of defeated opponents and, in that way, many new fixtures began.

Perhaps the most unusual fixture of the whole competition was the match Haig sponsored in 1976 between the Surrey side and an eleven selected from all the villages. Surrey, whose team included seven players with Test match experience, batted first. After Geoff Howarth, John Edrich and Graham Roope were back in the pavilion for modest scores, the county side never quite recovered and were all out for 150. The National Village XI owed most to the irresistible Terry Carter of Troon, whose 51 did most towards the six-wickets' win which the 'villagers' secured. Clearly, the game had been played in the best of spirits—as Haig would have wanted—and honour was satisfied.

A year later, in 1977, the sponsors felt they had done enough for the competition on which they had spent a considerable sum and they withdrew their connection with it but *The Cricketer* with some courage continued to run and finance it, offering a bottle of port to every bowler who did a hat-trick.

One side-effect was to take the magazine into the homes of village cricketers—a new departure for a paper which had traditionally been identified with the game at

Surrey v a National Village XI, 1976; village cricketers and the 'stars' are indistinguishable nowadays! (*John Haig & Co Ltd*)

first-class and town club level. In 1979, the brewers Samuel Whitbread Ltd took over the sponsorship of the competition and village cricketers quickly adjusted their drinking habits yet again, to their new benefactor.

Knock-out competitions at local level were also popular—though by no means an innovation. In Oxfordshire, a competition sponsored by the town club of Abingdon appealed to village clubs within the county. The final between Kennington and Moreton led the *Oxford Mail* to report that 'a superb display of attacking cricket from both sides saw Kennington scrape home by six runs against Moreton. The crowd was treated to a run-feast 250 in 36 overs—with the result uncertain to the last ball. Moreton delighted the crowd with its open aggressive play.'

Whatever doldrums the game might have fallen into in the 1960s had clearly vanished ten years later. As well as these knock-out competitions, village cricketers had thrown their energies into league cricket.

As we saw, before 1914 few village sides were in leagues. During the inter-war period there was some increase but the great 'growth' period was after 1945. Probably three-quarters of the villages of the 1970s belonged to a league of some sort and it would be tedious and lengthy to name even a fraction of them. Their origins may have been modest, such as the group of clubs in Essex who formed their own league with an entrance fee of 3d, or fiercely contested by clubs who did not want a league imposed on a long tradition of friendly cricket. One of the last strongholds of non-league cricket was Sussex where the proposal to introduce league cricket was first raised in 1969. One club circulated its fellow-members with a prepared list of arguments against, from which the following extracts are taken:

1 There is nothing wrong with the friendly competitive cricket which we at present play. Playing for points would tend to remove this friendly atmosphere.
2 Disruption to long-standing fixtures with clubs outside the area who would not participate would make the fixture secretary's task more difficult than at present. A league will dictate to a degree whom you play, and when.
3 Team selection will have its problems. The weaker player, who is sometimes selected to play because he is a good type, does a lot of hard work for the club, enjoys the beer and social atmosphere, will not get his place.
4 A deleterious effect will follow on spectator attendance at village cricket, where people have come to expect entertaining cricket, which is produced by variety in bowling (ie, the spin bowler), batting and field placing.
5 Few clubs in our standard of cricket are fortunate enough to be blessed with good umpires who can stand regularly. Can you imagine the effect between clubs who have been on the best of terms for years, when a few precious points are decided by a bad decision? These incidents happen at present, but are soon forgotten over a glass of beer.
6 As cricket has been played on Sussex village greens for more than two hundred years and enjoyed by generations of cricketers and spectators alike, it is difficult to appreciate that league cricket is wanted when it is considered that it will not do anything to improve the game.

As a summary of the arguments against leagues in village cricket, they cannot be bettered. Yet, ten years later, league cricket had come to the Sussex villages in the form of the County League and the Championship League while the newest league in the country, the Invitation League, began in 1979. Famous Sussex village sides as at Cuckfield, Lindfield, Steyning, Storrington and Henfield, battled in that new league that summer after (for many of them) two centuries of playing the game at 'friendly' level.

In travelling around while writing this book, I am left with the impression that

The adapted Trojan shooting brake with which Earlswood cut and rolled their field in the 1930s

before long competitive village cricket in leagues will be almost totally representative of the game at that level. The 'friendly' village side will find it harder to attract youngsters for whom the excitement of 'points' has much appeal.

Yet, 'points' or not, there is a pastoral charm about a village cricket match which is timeless. The church stands eternal, the pub claims antiquity and those who watch are the passing generations. Harassed young mothers cast care aside for an hour or two as their toddlers frolic safely in the long grass. Older wives catch up on the gossip of the week, clapping without discrimination when events on the field suggest it is their duty. Picnic teas appear as five o'clock approaches, and disappear by ten past. Grannies, over for the day, put tired youngsters to bed. Mums, wives and sweethearts make their way up for a drink with their menfolk. Halves of bitter and an hour or two of idleness; the smell of new-mown grass; a full moon picking out the silhouettes of houses and farmsteads; an endless reiteration of the afternoon's events; the cosiness of the community; a sight of well-known faces; it is not so much to ask. It has a touch of Paradise. Men and women in the outposts of Empire have dreamt of less.

Many factors have contributed to a vast improvement in the standards of village cricket squares. After 1919 mowing machines came to replace scythes. The Warwickshire club, Earlswood, cut and rolled their field in the 1930s with an adapted Trojan shooting brake to which rollers were fitted instead of wheels. Clubs playing in leagues were expected to provide wickets of good quality, and many did

'The committee, George, feel we ought to modernise, y'know. Update, get with it. Mechanical age, equality of the sexes and all that. We'll all miss you. Your sarcasm, your vulgarity, your unflagging idleness . . . GET LOST! (*Cartoon by Hargreaves*)

so, thanks to the work of devoted groundsmen. By the 1970s probably one village club in three was paying someone to work part-time on the square. Public money also became available through local authorities who were glad enough to have parish property looked after for them. The resources of the National Playing Fields Association and the Lord's Taverners helped with major capital grants and loans for projects involving laying new squares as well as building pavilions and buying machinery.

As the publicity given to the final rounds of the Haig and Whitbread National Competitions revealed to the British public at large, the village game has become 'professional' in the sense that it offers standards comparable with cricket at higher levels and far removed from the 'blacksmith and braces' image. The village cricketer has narrowed the gap between himself and the town clubs. This is especially true in captaincy, fielding and bowling. The defensive field-setting—so much a feature of the limited-overs game—is understood and practised by the village captain. His fielders (most of them!) perform with a high degree of athleticism. His bowlers, especially his seamers, will have a line and length that win respect from batsmen of a higher class.

It is less true so far as batting is concerned. A village side will have less batting 'in depth' than a town side. Fewer players will reveal a real range of shots. There will be more intuitive striking of the ball and less controlled defence. The natural instinct is to play across the line of the ball and the village cricketer, less tutored than his town counterpart, is more likely to do this.

Having said all this, we may notice some of the high scoring performances of today's village sides. Two hundred and fifty is regarded as a strong target to set the opposition. Among sides which set their opponents over 300 to get have been Canon Frome in Herefordshire, Sutton on the Hill in Derbyshire, Cookley in Worcestershire, Gowerton in South Wales, Temple Cloud in Gloucestershire and Aston Rowant and Moreton in Oxfordshire.

At least three cricketers made double centuries in the 1970s—Michael Hopkins for Cookley making 214 in 1978 while Trevor Botting of Balcombe in Sussex and Tim Cannon of Cokenach in Hertfordshire made cricket history on 15 May 1977 with double centuries on the same day.

This orgy of run-getting may also include Belford's first wicket stand of 255 while an unusual partnership was that of father and son who scored 196 for none for the Sussex village of Southwater against Amberley in 1978. George Blake made 78 not out and his son, Melvin, 99 not out before their captain declared the innings closed in time to dismiss Amberley. Another feat was the fourth wicket partnership of 249 between Nigel Broomfield, the British amateur squash champion, and Ken Stephens for Blackheath against Worplesdon in 1970.

One village side which made a huge score in the nineteenth century was Great Bentley in Essex whose 311 for nine in 1845 was impressive enough. Unfortunately, they batted all day! 'When can we have our bat?' is the plaintive cry of small boys when the big boy bats too long! The Bures' captain perhaps made the same plea but it was not answered for 112 years. Bures duly got their turn in 1957 and levelled the scores with five wickets down. Then came a hat-trick before they scraped the winning run with two wickets left.

Typical of the successful side of the 1970s is the Welsh club of Gowerton. There, in front of tall chimney stacks, a factory and a railway embankment, the game is played in a severe and businesslike way. 'The standard's very high', said a critical newcomer from Midlands' League cricket. The rugby players of Gowerton form a supporters' club—'Rentacrowd' they call themselves. There is passion and determination: enough to have taken Gowerton to Lord's twice and to emerge in 1975 as national village champions.

Village cricketers were able to entertain in 1976 the first team ever to come from Victoria, British Columbia to the United Kingdom. Sides such as Longparish in Hampshire, Sonning and Moreton in Oxfordshire, and Blackheath in Surrey provided the opposition. A year later, the Queen's Silver Jubilee gave an opportunity for village cricket to be part of a community pattern of celebrations, with sports, bonfires, old people's parties and fireworks. And village cricketers still have their age-old problems. Recently an Oxfordshire side had to keep asking 'Can we have our ball back?' as a nearby house-owner (albeit the captain's aunt) collected balls which sailed over her garden wall. The dispute eventually found its way to the local courts.

Clubs are naturally proud of the players whose family links go back some generations. They recall the Goodwins, father and son, secretaries of Langley in Buckinghamshire, for ninety years; the three Hunts (grandfather, father and son) who turned out for Earlswood in 1940—spanning playing careers from 1886 to 1979; the five Till brothers who played for Sessay in Yorkshire, while their sister scored, their father was the president and their grandfather watched—recalling that *his* father remembered scoring by notches. Most clubs have their 'Mr Chips' whose loyalty, through good and bad times, has held them together.

It is the fashion in present-day cricket to have a Man of the Match. Let me select Bob Rogers as my village cricketer of the twentieth century. He made his debut for Farnham Common in Buckinghamshire in 1909 and soon after began work as an aircraft mechanic working on the Avros used by the Royal Flying Corps. He flew with Sir John Alcock who was to become the first British pilot to cross the Atlantic non-stop, and he completed a lifetime's connection with the aircraft industry by flying in Concorde shortly after playing in his last cricket match.

Bob Rogers' cricket was played variously for Farnham Common, Ottershaw and

Bob Rogers with the ball with which he took five wickets in five balls on August Bank Holiday, 1923

In 1957 an entire *Punch* staff XI took on Blackheath; Bernard Hollowood, editor and captain, is in the centre

West Byfleet in Surrey. When he retired from work at the age of sixty-five he moved to Dorset and joined the Verwood and Ferndown Club. His career was principally as a bowler but he was a good enough batsman to have a highest score of 136 not out, to make at least one half-century in most years and to score two centuries after he became a grandfather.

As a bowler Bob Rogers took nearly 2,000 wickets which included spoiling (for the opposition) an August bank holiday match in 1923 by taking eight wickets for 11. He hit the stumps on every occasion, and his performance included five wickets in five consecutive balls. He must have been something of a nightmare to Ottershaw's annual opponents whose wickets he secured on fifty-two occasions in the next six bank holiday matches.

He recalled his cricket memories of seventy years ago:

> To travel in 1909 we had no bicycles, coaches, only two cars in the village and sometimes we had to ride in the coal cart. The rough out-field we played on never saw a mowing machine or a roller. The vicar gave us good advice. I have never forgotten his words. 'The bat is made to hit the ball, not stop it. Never put your legs in front of the wicket to be given out lbw, there are enough ways of getting out without giving yourself up.'

'. . . their sons put up the numbers on the board.' Scoreboard operators in the 1960s still wore shorts

He attributed his ability to play for so long to a lifetime of no smoking, eating his own honey and keeping rheumatism at bay with bee-stings.

Bob Rogers spent his working life in the aircraft industry. Among a variety of occupations, village cricketers since 1919 have included a trainer of greyhounds, the leader in a London orchestra, a deputy chairman of the Inland Revenue, a Belgian count, a river pilot and a mole and rabbit catcher. Authors and writers are frequent performers. J. M. Barrie formed a team of authors called the Allakabarries. H. E. Bates played for Chart in Kent, Conan Doyle for Grayshott in Surrey and Hugh de Sélincourt captained and gave literary immortality to Storrington. Henry Blyth captained Rottingdean and Bernard Hollowood edited *Punch* and played for Blackheath. John Galsworthy was in the Bury side in Sussex. In front of castles and palaces, in the lee of mountains, by grandstands made of civil war earthworks, before Norman churches, near the tang of the sea and the fumes of the stack, by manor house and tithe barn, the village cricketers have played their games and their ladies have watched.

Where, without those ladies, would village cricket be? They will be found the length and breadth of Britain, making cakes, cutting sandwiches, putting on the kettle, serving tea and washing up afterwards. Their husbands are playing and their sons put up the numbers on the board. All this may be regarded as 'standard procedure'.

Those prepared to work bonus-time (but, of course, there are no bonus payments, or payments at all) may be found selling home-made produce (a sort of WI market in the pavilion), organising bingo, running the bar, setting up the barbecue, or simply scoring—a five-hour stint watching every ball bowled.

Then there is a 'de luxe' class who have been found on the club selection committee, umpiring (one, a grandmother) and acting as groundswomen (one lady services all the club machinery). Such ladies may turn their hand to first aid or painting, or to washing, mending and ironing players' kit. One would cut the players' hair in the pavilion when rain stopped play.

A lady who described herself as a dedicated cricket wife, reckoning she gave

'Marry me and do the teas for the club on Saturdays' (*Cartoon by Hargreaves*)

Ladies' cricket at the village of Colwall in Herefordshire where there has been an annual festival for over thirty years; a waiting batsman is getting on with her knitting! (*Berrow's Newspapers*)

seventy hours a week to the village club, allowed me to quote her remarks. 'I never knew I was marrying into cricket. They're the biggest shower of doing-nothings. They only think of cricket. I never drink tea myself, never. After a few years they gave me a presentation. A tin with one of those Constable paintings on the outside. Very nice. A kind thought. Inside there were seventy-two tea bags. They'd never even noticed I didn't drink the stuff.' I would have liked to ask her more. 'I've no time, dear. Got to do their teas and run their bar for them.'

The ladies even get a game themselves sometimes though there is not the village rivalry as in years gone by. Its interest has moved from the south to the north where there are clubs at Bedale, Burton Leonard, Hutton Bonville, Leyburn, Roecliffe and Sessay. Sides can also be found in the East Midlands and in the Thames Valley and a notable newcomer is the Kimble Ladies village side in Buckinghamshire largely full of some very young lady cricketers with a lifetime of playing in front of them. In the grand tradition of Hambledon of old, there is a link between the village and the national game. Rachel Heyhoe-Flint, the former

England captain, took many representative sides in the 1970s to play against men's village teams. Such contests could have interesting sidelines. At Warninglid in Sussex, the vicar let the ladies use the vicarage as a changing room and in return expected them at evensong after the game. The men went too!

What was the very last village fixture of the decade of the 1970s? It took place on 26 December 1979 between the Northern Cricket Society and North Leeds. This annual Boxing Day match, which began in 1949, is played between the NCS and varying village sides in Yorkshire; it has never been cancelled—whatever the weather. The teams have turned out in sunshine which would not disgrace a May day and in snow which had to be swept away after every ball. Other villages have had their occasional games. Only the Yorkshiremen guarantee play.

The village cricketer of the 1970s was a different person from his predecessors. John Arlott has written: 'Village cricket is a serious matter. Once it was considered

Family of British mammals during hibernation (*Cartoon by Hargreaves*)

Boxing Day cricket in Yorkshire; the Alwoodley innings has just ended. It is not a Haig tie but one hopes that whisky is available in the pavilion (*Yorkshire Post*)

clever to make jokes about it. Villagers do not think village cricket is funny. They do not play it for fun. They play it to win.' A hard judgement? John Arlott has seen the game in his native Hampshire. He is knowledgeable about past traditions and folklore and about the village cricket of the south-east with its Kentish origins. And he is a realist. He recognises change. 'Village cricket is not what it was: nothing is.'

But the names remain the same, and so many of them appeal to the imagination. Conjure up a picture of these village finalists at Lord's one day: Misken Manor v. Catherine-de-Barnes, Upton St Leonards v. Havering-atte-Bower, Steeple Norden v. Great and Little Tew, and Backworth Percy v. Hinton in the Hedges.

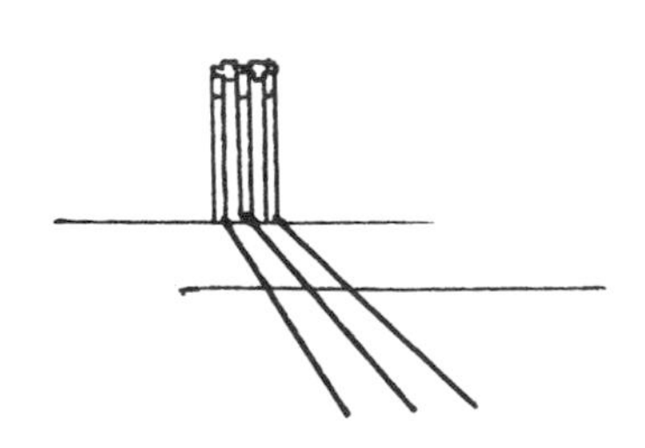

3
YORKSHIRE SPECTATOR

Headingley on an August Saturday offered the refreshing sight of crowds pouring in an hour before play began to see a three-day county match. Discerning Yorkshire men and women made for their favourite seats, settling down to watch their own homespun opening batsmen, Richard Lumb and Kevin Sharp, face the Sussex attack.

A Yorkshire county cricketer, born as he must be in the county, has made his way up a hard school. He has played league cricket at various levels and was probably first spotted by some zealous county 'scout' when he was a twelve-year-old. The process is so thorough that I asked a former player why Yorkshire didn't win every tournament going. 'Because every time they play another county they play the rest of the world,' was the reply. One day a West Indian or Pakistani, born and bred in Bradford, will wear the cap with the white rose.

Anthony Woodhouse, my Yorkshire host and possessor of one of the greatest cricket libraries in the world, bore me away from Headingley at the lunch interval. We drove westwards to Halifax through the West Riding of Yorkshire where coal and cloth have dominated the scene and where mill, factory, foundry and mine have provided employment for countless folk. Presently we came to the tiny village of Copley, once the home of Lawrence Sterne, the author. A vast Victorian viaduct carried the main railway line from Bradford to Preston and parallel to it ran the line from Leeds to Liverpool—two great arteries of communication which bore the freight of Yorkshire's prosperity in the Industrial Revolution. Between them lay the cricket ground set in the Dales with a backcloth of horse chestnuts and beeches. A very old man was watching the Copley men in the field. They said he had once hit a ball on to the viaduct. He smiled at the recollection. The passage of years had lengthened the hit and lowered the viaduct. There was no one now to dispute his claim, and no one could match it either.

As you entered the ground you could see the coal shutes, where the pony carts collected the coal that dropped through a shute from the railway high above and brought it to the nearby mill. Once there had been that mill and its cottages and precious little else—no pub, no church or chapel. When church and chapel came it spelt trouble for t'cricket. Parson and preacher got together and threatened to withdraw their membership subscriptions if cricket were played on a Sunday.

Three Yorkshire and England opening batsmen, all of whom made one hundred centuries in the first-class game and who began their cricket in the villages—Geoff Boycott, Herbert Sutcliffe and Sir Leonard Hutton at Headingley in 1977 (*Ken Kelly*)

By now, Copley had taken three of Crossley's Carpets wickets for 13. Both teams stood at the top of the Halifax League and points were vital. The Copley ladies looked pleased as they prepared the cold meat and salad for tea. 'You get a pot of tea, cakes, meat and salad for thirty pence,' they said. Barbara Smith had been preparing cricket teas all her life. Her father-in-law had played for Copley before the First World War, her husband was president, her son was out there fielding, and her son-in-law had taken the game up in self-defence.

Crossley's Carpets gradually pieced together an innings. Someone came round with a hat as the opener reached his 50: that afternoon he probably took home £2 or £3.

After the First World War the club had bought the village ground for £100 from Benders, the Yorkshire brewers. The money was borrowed from the bank, and the ladies raised £10 a year for ten years. All of them were made vice-presidents for their efforts. 'It's the ladies who have come up with all the ideas for raising money in this club,' said Barbara, 'for the last fifty years,' she added.

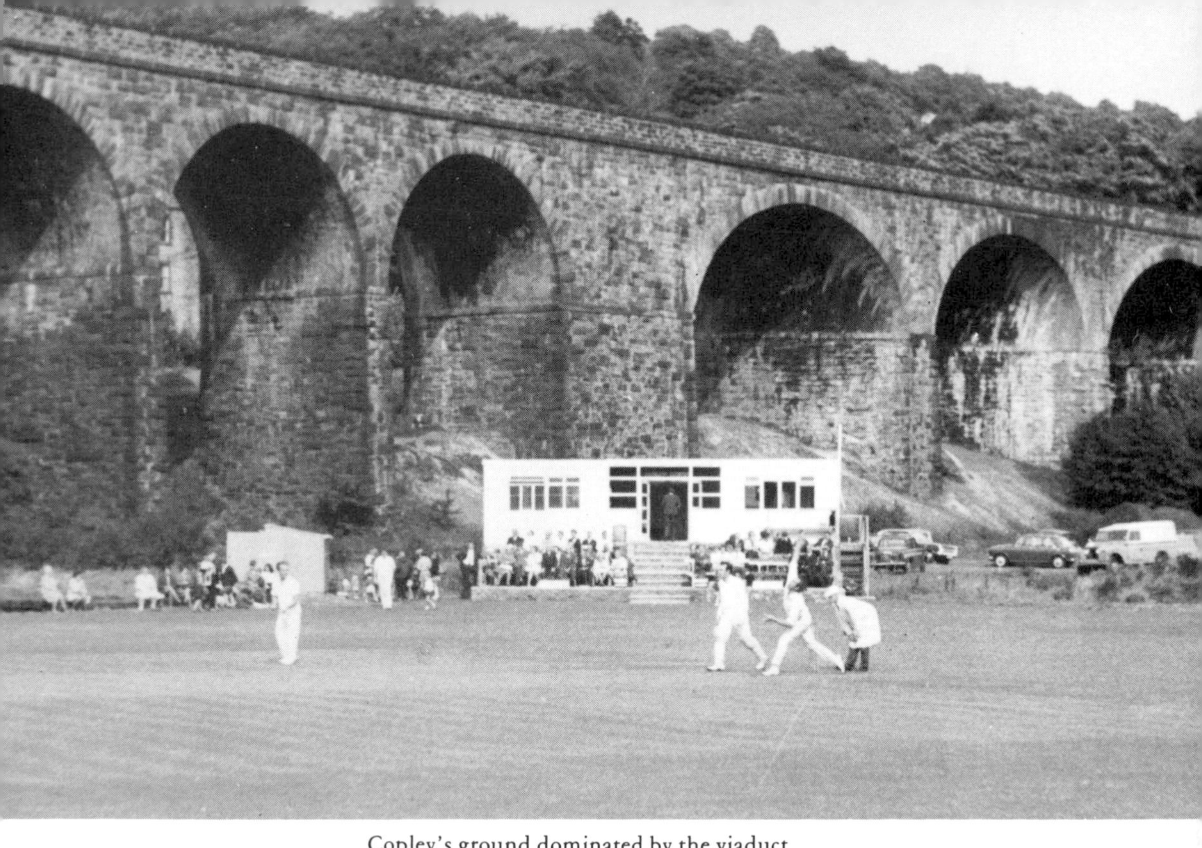

Copley's ground dominated by the viaduct

The Copley side in 1914; Barbara Smith's father-in-law is captain

'Wake up, Boycott—you're in' (*Cartoon by Giles, London Express Service*)

Crossley's Carpets passed the hundred with five wickets down, as Copley's policeman came on to bowl. No one in Copley earned his living in the carpet trade, and the old cloth mill no longer existed. Copley was a village of new model houses built of brick, housing people who commuted to Halifax to work in banks or building societies. There was local employment in the building trade and in highways' maintenance. After Crossley's were dismissed for 139, the village doctor opened Copley's batting. Old Frank watched him with a critical eye, as indeed he might. Frank had watched men going to the wicket at Copley since the turn of the century when he earned 3s 6d a week at the mill as a lad. He had watched men go off to two wars—'they kept me back on the railways,' he said and produced a picture of the Copley side in 1914. A man from that small community of 700 had won a Victoria Cross.

Frank had brought his own tea and ate it apart while the Copley and Crossley's players set about Barbara's meat and salad. Copley could enjoy their tea; their target was 139, no great score on the tiny ground. 'There were five points for t'taking,' said Roy Smith, Barbara's husband, as we drove off past the war-time munition store, skirted Rochdale Canal, noticed the old Co-op with a bonus of 4s in the £, and the gaunt neo-Gothic church, tall, dark and impressive, built by the mill-owner for the proper occupation of the workers on a Sunday.

Down the Rochdale road, in the valley of the River Cragg, and on past Sowerby was Triangle who were playing Siddal. Here were two village teams struggling to avoid relegation to the second division of the Halifax League. There can be few smaller grounds in England than Grassy Bottom Triangle. It lies wedged between the River Ryburn and a steep hillside of beech and elm trees. A lad in waders is paid 50 pence a match to fish out balls. At one end, high, overpowering and redundant, stands the old mill, once owned by Colonel Thomas Morris.

Thomas Morris as a schoolboy had watched Triangle's first match in October 1862 when they had made 74 and dismissed Sowerby twice for a grand total of 65. As a young man he had brought his school and university friends to play a match against Triangle every Whit-Monday. As an old man, he had purchased Grassy Bottom at a cost of £650 and had handed over the freehold to a body of trustees, so long as cricket was played there. That was in the 1920s. Colonel Morris's mill at Triangle no longer operated but the nearby mill of Stansfield was still closely associated with Triangle cricket. The managing director was chairman of Grassy Bottom's trustees and president of the cricket club.

So long as there was someone to cut the wicket, no Triangle player need worry about the club's future. Relegation seemed less remote as they dismissed Siddal for 118. Triangle and Siddal sat down to their own meat and salad tea. I had just managed to eat the beginning and end of two cricket teas in one afternoon.

Some preferred something stronger than tea. A well-stocked bar was doing a brisk trade, of which Colonel Morris might not altogether have approved. He had given up the licence of the old White Bear in Triangle which his father had held and replaced the pub with a reading, smoking and recreation room. Therein lay two important Victorian principles—temperance and education. To reduce drinking among working men and to encourage the rudiments of learning among those who would use the new technology of the mill satisfied both the moralist and the businessman in Morris.

From that reading room had sprung the cricket club whose constitution, revised in 1977, still declared an intention to offer its members 'mental and moral encouragement and rational recreation'. Part of that recreation extended beyond mere cricket. Morris's Whit-Monday matches were succeeded by entertainments on a larger scale which drew crowds of over two thousand. Cricket would be supported by penny-farthing cycling competitions and athletic contests, backed up by a brass band and followed by a dance.

The money from such functions gave Triangle the resources with which to employ their first professional, soon to be followed by Frank Scott who, they said, never bowled a wide or a no-ball.

Scott helped Triangle to win the Halifax Cup in 1903, he and his partner securing the 25 needed by the last pair to defeat Halifax 'A'. A few weeks earlier that Triangle side had made the long journey to Norden in Lancashire, a match of

Cricket at Triangle: 'at one end, high, overpowering and redundant, stands the old mill'

such interest that the team took two homing pigeons to send back the scores. The first pigeon flew back with the news that Triangle had put on 190 for the first wicket.

Although there was no professional now in the Triangle side, there was surely the money for one. Village cricket is big business when the bar receipts for the year exceed £5,000, while income from the sale of paper and old cartons from the neighbouring mill brings a further £500. Members paid £156 and vice-presidents £7. The age of benevolent patrons was dying fast. Gate money had brought in £29 the previous season. The spectators were getting their money's worth as Triangle set off to chase Siddal's 118, with 20 on the board in the first four overs, and the net boy busily employed in the river. Those spectators were taking the game pretty seriously. Quite a crowd sat round, fiercely partisan and well informed. Even the children had to sit still and appreciate the cricket which they had been brought along to watch. On Triangle's small ground there wasn't anywhere else for them to

'. . . and besides being bowlers our chaps are a batting side, right down to number eleven . . .'
(*Cartoon by Hargreaves*)

go. Here, at any rate, cricket was for ever as Colonel Morris had stipulated. Its immediate future seemed in no doubt as the Triangle batsmen coasted home to a seven wickets' victory over Siddal.

Next week they would be away to Mackintosh's, the toffee people who offered employment to some of those redundant in recent mill closures, and then at home to Crossley's Carpets. It was time for me to return to Copley to find out how they had fared against the carpet men. Alas! Copley had crumbled to defeat and were all out for 89. Mackintosh's had also lost that afternoon, and so had nearby Sowerby.

Among the most famous of Yorkshire village sides playing that Saturday were Lascelles Hall who finished their game some 70 runs behind Slaithwaite. The two clubs were meeting in the Huddersfield and District League on Lascelles Hall's beautiful little ground commanding a view of the Yorkshire hills.

Cricket at Lascelles had first begun when some lads had trespassed with bat and ball on to the estate of Mr Joseph Walker. Instead of some stern Victorian punishment being meted out, they were awarded 'playing rights', which the club enjoyed for some thirty years until it was decided to construct its present ground. Men either paid 3s 6d a day for labour or worked themselves producing a ground good enough on which to play the United-England XI professionals in August 1867. Twenty-two men from the village of weavers defeated the visiting professionals by 6 runs. Six years later the village triumphed over Yorkshire by 146 runs in a three-day match. Indeed, Lascelles Hall had become the nursery of Yorkshire's own side so that between 1861 and the end of the nineteenth century twenty-one Lascelles men were picked for the county. They included William Bates, who toured Australia three times in the 1880s, and Allan Hill, who once took a hat-trick which included 'W.G'.

Perhaps a clue to the cricketing successes of the small village community lies in a letter written by Edward Hirst who played for the club in the 1870s and 1880s and occasionally for Yorkshire.

> Whatever small measure of success I may have achieved in the cricket field I owe to the splendid practice I got day after day in the evenings on the beautiful wickets at Lascelles Hall, with some of the best bowlers in England bowling at me. If a man or boy could not learn to play cricket at Lascelles Hall he was past praying for.

The Minute Books are evidence of the efficiency and discipline of the club:

1862 That the preparing of the ground be got up in the best style at any expense.

1865 That Joseph Thewlis as bowler to the club perform the functions of captain during practice hours, and that any member declining to conform to his orders shall not be entitled to his innings.

The men did not have it all their own way at Pudsey; this is the Married Ladies' XI of Pudsey Britannia in the 1920s

There are also quainter items such as that in 1869 indicating that a member paying £1 or more might go in next. In 1873 a Minute noted that the eleventh place in the team would be filled by ballot, while five years later 10s spending money was provided by the club for away matches.

Lascelles Hall's twentieth-century career has been more prosaic, a record of satisfactory though not outstanding performances in the Huddersfield League, with the championship coming their way three times, and the Sykes Cup (the league knock-out trophy) another three.

As we drove back through Bradford in the evening, stopping to buy the 'Pink' evening paper with all the day's results, I asked about cricket at the Pudseys. Pudsey St Lawrence, the club from which Sir Leonard Hutton had come, still flourished and had just beaten Baildon in the Bradford League. But Pudsey Britannia—the nursery of that other great Yorkshire and England opening bat, Herbert Sutcliffe—had closed in 1967 after more than a century of playing in the Bradford and (later) the Leeds Leagues. But a happy ending to the fortunes of Britannia's old ground was in sight. Pudsey Congs had bought it during the summer and were busy restoring the ground. The hope was that cricket would return to Pudsey Britannia in 1980.

Nearby, playing also in the Bradford League that afternoon, were East Bierley

Both the 1979 finalists find an unusual way to arrive at Lord's, and East Brierley take the national title back to Yorkshire (*Allsport Photographic*)

who had beaten Bankfoot by sixty runs. If Lascelles Hall were a club with a past, East Bierley were one with a future. Exactly a year later, in August 1979, they were at Lord's taking 216 for four off the Welsh village of Ynysygerwyn to become the first winners of the Samuel Whitbread national village competition. And if you had to be born in Yorkshire to play for Yorkshire, East Bierley were less particular —their star performer at Lord's was West Indian Clive Defoe.

Yorkshire produced the champion village in August 1979 and in the same week another Yorkshire village got into the record-books. Until Cawood bowled their first ball which went for four byes and passed the Dringhouses' total of 2, no side had ever won a match before without bat touching ball. On current form, Cawood were not considering investing in any new bats, an official told me.

Back to the 'Pink' paper: all over Yorkshire that day several hundreds of village clubs, from mill and colliery, from Sunday school and chapel, from working men's clubs and woolsorters' institutes, were playing cricket and celebrating afterwards in close, tightly-knit communities. In Copley they were holding Tom Edwards' retirement party. Yorkshire village cricket is a family affair. I had visited the family and been made most welcome.

4
EIGHTEENTH-CENTURY VILLAGE

Thousands had come by coach and four, by waggon, on horseback or on foot to watch Hambledon play cricket at Broad-Halfpenny Down. There was plenty of incentive! Richard Nyren had laid in a stock of excellent wine and 'a sufficient quantity of beef, chicken and tarts'. There was a tent for the ladies covered in green baize, and they were promised as much comfort 'as if they were in their own dressing room.'

As the match progressed to a climax, the comfort of tents was forgotten as everyone crowded round the green, 'patiently and anxiously watching every turn of fate in the game, as if the event had been the meeting of two armies to decide their liberty.'

Hambledon had the support of the great majority of spectators. Every time a Hambledon man made a hit they would be 'baying away in pure Hampshire—"Go hard! Tich and turn! Tich and turn!"' And with ten runs to get old farmers leant forward upon their staves, Sir Horatio Mann cut down the daisies with a stick and the whole multitude was still. When the match was won, it was time for punch 'that would stand on end, that would make a cat speak' and ale 'that would flare like turpentine.'

Darkness fell, the crowds stumbled home through the Meon valley along uncertain Hampshire lanes and Richard Nyren could relax. He had had a mild exchange of words with Sir Horatio during the day but he had been 'proved to be in the right' and Mann had shaken him heartily by the hand. He knew where he stood with the nobility and gentlemen in the cricketing world, 'he could differ with a superior without trenching upon his dignity, or losing his own.' Nyren had come to Hambledon from Slindon in the 1760s and for a generation he was 'the chosen general of all the matches, ordering and directing the whole.' The 'general' was captain and secretary of the Hambledon club and landlord of the village hostelry, the Bat and Ball. He was, wrote his son, 'the finest specimen of the thorough-bred old English yeoman'.

Richard Nyren's son, John, had watched the Hambledon games as a boy, and it is his memories of them which appeared as 'The Cricketers of my Time' published in his *The Young Cricketer's Tutor* fifty years later. As John Arlott has observed, the book is the story of 'the first phase of cricket of which any valid contemporary view exists' in its portraits of the men who played in the Hambledon team.

The best batsman was John Small of Petersfield who began life as a shoemaker, later became a gamekeeper and a draper and, as a sideline, made and sold bats and balls. Outside his house hung the sign:

Here lives John Small
Makes bat and ball,
Pitch a wicket, play at cricket
With any man in England.

He was also a violinist and played the double bass. To the Duke of Dorset's gift of a violin, he returned a pair of bats. John Nyren thought highly of Small's cricketing abilities—fast between the wickets, quick in the field and an admirable user of his wrists in batting. When he died, these lines commemorated him:

Here lies, bowled out by Death's unerring ball,
A cricketer renowned, by name John Small,
But though his name was Small, yet great his fame,
For nobly did he play the noble game;
His life was like his innings, long and good.
Full ninety summers he had death withstood.
At length the ninetieth winter came, when (fate
Not leaving him one solitary mate)
This last of Hambledonians, Old John Small,
Gave up his bat and ball, his leather, wax and all.

A match on Broad-Halfpenny Down in 1777

John Nyren, author of 'The Cricketers of my Time' (*MCC*)

The club was well served behind the stumps by Tom Sueter, a builder and carpenter. Nyren admired his 'coolness and nerve' as much as he did his tenor voice in the club-room afterwards. Since 'nothing went by him' one wonders what work his long-stop, George Leer, a brewer by trade, had to do. But Nyren reminds us that long-stop often did duty as slip and 'to the swiftest bowling ever known'. Leer sang counter tenor; he and Sueter entertained the customers of the Bat and Ball with their glees. Behind wicket-keeper and long-stop there was cover-long-stop, a position usually filled by Noah Mann. Sometimes Sueter and Leer would miss the ball deliberately so that unwary batsmen would be tempted into a quick single, only to be dismissed by Mann's quick return to the stumps. Mann, who died tragically in front of his own fireside when sparks ignited his clothes, after an over-indulgent evening's drinking, was a shoemaker turned publican who would ride twenty miles from North Chapel in Sussex to practise on Tuesday evenings. 'To show the amenity in which the men of lower grade lived in those good old days with their superiors,' John Nyren related how his father, Richard, 'the link between the patricians and the plebeians in our community,' approached Mann's namesake, Sir Horatio, to become godfather to Noah's son. 'By this simple act of graceful humanity (he) hooked for life the heart of poor Noah Mann.'

Besides Richard Nyren himself, the bowlers included William Barber, a Sussex shoemaker, Thomas Brett, a farmer from Catherington, and William Hogsflesh from Southwick. There was also Lamborn the shepherd's son, who practised bowling while tending his sheep, a 'plain spoken little bumpkin' whose off-breaks were too good for the Duke of Dorset. 'Tedious near you, sir', he exclaimed in his broad Hampshire dialect.

There was John Wells, the baker from Farnham, 'a creature of an unflawed integrity, plain, simple and candid; uncompromising yet courteous, civil and deferential, yet no cringer'; John Freemantle, a master-builder from Alresford and his younger brother Andrew, a carpenter who 'could be depended upon, whatever he might undertake, whether in cricket or in other worldly dealings'; Richard Francis, a gamekeeper from Surrey; Peter Stewart, a shoemaker and the club humorist; Tom Taylor from Ropley who got his runs by cutting the ball; and James Aylward, a farmer from Warnford who once made 167.

Nyren introduces the Walker brothers, farmer's sons from Thursley, with one of his unabashed social judgements:

> Now for those anointed clod stumpers, the Walkers, Tom and Harry. Never sure came two such unadulterated rustics into a civilised community. How strongly are the figures of the men (of Tom's in particular) brought to my mind when they first presented themselves to the club upon Windmill Down. Tom's hard, ungainly, scrag-of-mutton frame; wilted, apple-john face, his long spider legs, as thick at the ankles as at the hips, and

The Bat and Ball at Hambledon (*MCC*)

The Hambledon side from sketches made by George Shepherd in the 1790s; on the left of the middle row is Tom Walker 'who moved like the rude machinery of a steam engine' while David Harris, top right, bowled 'with a graceful curve of the arm' (*MCC*)

perfectly straight all the way down—for the embellishment of a calf in Tom's leg Dame Nature had considered would be wanton superfluity. Tom was the driest and most rigid-limbed chap I ever knew, his skin was like the rind of an old oak, and as sapless. He moved like the rude machinery of a steam engine in the infancy of construction, and when he ran, every member seemed ready to fly to the four winds. He toiled like a tar on horseback.

But Nyren concedes their abilities. Tom 'was the coolest, the most imperturbable fellow in existence, whether he was only practising or whether the game was in a critical stage, he was the same phlegmatic, unmoved man—the Washington of cricketers'. Both brothers were valuable batsmen while Tom pioneered round-arm bowling which Nyren condemned as detrimental to the game.

His greatest praise was for William Beldam and David Harris. William Beldam, most of whose later life was spent at Tilford, was 'the best batter of his own, or perhaps any age'. He was a farmer's son who had learnt his early cricket from Harry Hall, a gingerbread baker, in Farnham. Beldam played relatively little at Hambledon itself, but his career spanned thirty-five seasons surviving into the 'camera' age and he was the only Hambledon cricketer to be photographed. At the age of eighty-six, in 1852, he walked seven miles to watch a match.

> David Harris was a potter from Crookham, and a bowler. It would be difficult to convey in writing an accurate idea of the grand effect of Harris's bowling; they only who have played against him can fully appreciate it. His attitude when preparing for his run previously to delivering the ball would have made a beautiful study for the sculptor. Phidias would certainly have taken him for a model. First of all, he stood erect like a soldier at drill; then with a graceful curve of the arm, he raised the ball to his forehead, and drawing back his right foot, started off with his left. The calm look and general air of the man were uncommonly striking, and from this series of preparations he never deviated. I am sure that from this simple account of his manner, all my countrymen who were acquainted with his play will recall him to their minds. His mode of delivering the

William Beldam 'the best batter of his own, or perhaps any age' as George Shepherd drew him and as photographed as an old man (*MCC*)

ball was very singular. He would bring it from under the arm by a twist, and nearly as high as his armpit, and with action push it, as it were, from him. How it was that the balls acquired the velocity they did by this mode of delivery I could never comprehend.

These were the local heroes who entertained the crowds at Broad-Halfpenny Down and, after 1782, at Windmill Down—a smaller ground but less bleak and nearer to the village inn!

But the Hambledon men were village cricketers with a difference. They were players whose talents had been spotted by members of the Hambledon Club and who were retained to play for that club. In an age of difficult communications they travelled from surrounding villages and towns to appear for Hambledon and were remunerated for their efforts. The accounts show that Small, Brett, Sueter and Leer, for example, were paid in May 1775 'for practising'. A player might get between 3s and 4s a day (and pay 3d fine if late), far better payment than the 1s 9d earned for a day's work by an agricultural worker.

John Small, as a craftsman, would hope to earn 2s 6d a day. The poor of the eighteenth century struggled to exist but the Hambledon village cricketers, as depicted in John Nyren's pages, give no hint of poverty or destitution. They were well rewarded for their prowess.

The Hambledon Club was, in fact, a gentleman's club. Between 1772 and 1796 it had 157 'gentlemen subscribers' of whom fifteen were noblemen or closely related to the peerage, twenty-one were clergymen and the remainder 'gentlemen' —only two of whom admitted to being in trade—one was a local draper and the other supplied wines to the club!

The members paid a subscription of two or three guineas, turned up to matches and wined and dined themselves well. In 1791, for example, subscriptions brought in an income of £129 3s 0d. The outlay was £106 5s 3d of which £65 14s 3d was used to pay players. The remainder went on hiring a tent, renting Windmill Down, printing, and on settling Richard Nyren's incidental expenses.

Nyren, as secretary, was very much the club servant. He was always styled Nyren in the Minutes without the prefix 'Mr'. 'The Gentlemen present have thought proper to allow Nyren two shillings a head for each dinner instead of one shilling,' recommended one Minute. The Minutes indicate clearly the social side of the club and the distinction between members and players.

25 May 1773 Ordered that the Stewards procure three dozen of Madeira at 40s from Mr Smith.
26 July 1785 At this meeting Mr Woolls and Mr Blackgrave were duly elected. Ordered that John and James Wells, William and George Beldam be considered as players belonging to this club and be paid their expenses when they came to play at the discretion of the Stewards.

Cricket at Moulsey Hurst in the 1780s (*MCC*)

Being men of the eighteenth century much of the interest of the members came from betting on the matches in which the sums won and lost made the annual subscription look like small change. John Nyren thought that £500 might be normal stake money placed by some of the richer members on a match.

While none of the village players ever attended meetings of the club, according to the Minutes, some of the gentlemen subscribers played for it. The Duke of Dorset played sometimes and as a ballad in the *Gentleman's Magazine* in 1773 reveals:

He firmly stands with bat upright
And strikes with his athletic might,
Sends forth the ball across the mead,
And scores six notches for the deed.

Sir Horatio Mann, 'a batter of great might', also appeared occasionally for Hambledon, while the appearance of the Earl of Winchelsea at a match on Windmill Down on 14 July 1789 has symbolic importance. The noble earl had the misfortune to be dismissed for nought in both innings. On the very day when an English aristocrat could accept such humbling treatment at the hands of William Bullen, a commoner and a fast bowler from Deptford, the mob in Paris was storming the Bastille. Across the Channel revolution had broken out. As the historian G. M. Trevelyan has observed, 'If the French *noblesse* had been capable of playing cricket with their peasants, their chateaux would never have been burnt.'

The judgement is simplistic but not without some substance. Cricketers such as those at Hambledon, in John Nyren's view, prevented 'the structure of society from becoming disjointed'. Village cricket was one of the safety valves against a

Hambledon played England once again—in 1908 (*MCC*)

repetition of French events in England—which the Prime Minister, William Pitt, genuinely feared in the 1790s. But the French Revolution denied the Duke of Dorset the chance of being the first Englishman to sponsor an England tour to France! As British Ambassador to that country, he invited an eleven to play in Paris. At Dover, the tourists met the ambassador himself, hastily recalled from a country in revolutionary turmoil.

The Hambledon Club played against villages in Hampshire and Sussex such as Henfield, Titchfield, Alresford and Odiham. But they also played matches against no less opposition than England, besides matches against Surrey and Kent. On fifty-one occasions Hambledon played England. That such an anomaly could take place is explained simply by the fact that the Hambledon members were excellent 'talent spotters'! Despite a fire in 1825 which destroyed many Hambledon records, we know something of these matches from various contemporary newspapers.

On that historic day, 4 July 1776, when the British American colonies declared their independence in far-off Philadelphia, Hambledon played England at Broad-Halfpenny Down. The village was dismissed for 87 in their first innings while England replied with 163—the Duke of Dorset scoring 34 of them. Hambledon recovered in their second innings, making 221 with a half-century from John Small and 36 from their captain, Richard Nyren. England struggled to a four-wickets' win.

A match at Broad-Halfpenny Down between the club and Surrey produced 754 runs and a large second-innings total of 357 (J. Small 136) by Hambledon. The club's game with Kent at Windmill Down in July 1783 ended in a tie but 'it was discovered afterwards that the scorer, whose method was to cut a notch on a stick for every run, and to cut every tenth notch longer, had, by mistake, marked in one place the eleventh notch instead of the tenth. The stick was afterwards produced; but the other scorer could not or would not produce his.' The error denied Kent victory.

In 1777 there were six contests between Hambledon and England. The first game, in June 1777, must have represented Hambledon's greatest achievement. After England had been dismissed for 166, largely due to the bowling of Brett, Hambledon replied with 403 (Aylward 167, Sueter 46, Nyren 37). England were dismissed for 69 at their second attempt, leaving Hambledon winners by an innings and 168 runs.

Not all Hambledon's matches were eleven-a-side contests. Many were single-wicket ones in which up to six players participated on each side. Hambledon, for example, played England at Moulsey Hurst in Surrey in 1781 winning by 78 runs while the late withdrawal of David Harris from a single-wicket match against Kent in 1789 changed the betting odds.

No village cricket club rose to fame so sharply or fell so suddenly. The great days of the Hambledon Club lay between 1770 and 1790. By 1795 they were over. John Nyren attributed the decline to the departure in 1791 of his father, Richard—'the head and right arm were gone'. But others had gone too. Some of the 'gentlemen subscribers' had left to fight in the French wars, described in the Minutes as having 'gone to sea'. Another member, said a thinly-erased Minute, had 'gone to the Devil'! Attendance of members had fallen so much that out of nine meetings in 1795 between May and September, four had no attenders at all. There were also problems in getting members' subscriptions.

As for the players, they gradually abandoned the obscure Hampshire village and took their professional skills to London where the attractions of the game had increased with the foundation of the Marylebone Cricket Club in 1787. By the end of the eighteenth century Hambledon village cricket was no more. A later generation would put Broad-Halfpenny Down to the plough, but village cricket returned to the Down in the twentieth century and it is there today.

5
WEST COUNTRY SPECTATOR

It is possible, on leaving the Thames Valley, to persuade yourself when you reach Wantage that you are already in the West Country. Alfred, King of the West Saxons, was born there and his statue stands in the market-place. Soon the White Horse cut out on the landscape of the Lambourn Downs takes you back to the Iron Age, centuries before Alfred, or Lambourn race horses, or, indeed, cricketers. But the White Horse gave its name to a pleasant little village cricket club founded at the King Alfred's Head in Wantage just a hundred years ago. They played the game 'according to Lillywhite's rules' and you could buy a copy of them for a shilling. You could also buy third-class membership of the Vale of the White Horse Cricket Club for the same sum, make a considered decision to be a second-class member for 1s 6d and purchase first-class membership for 2s. The new Great Western Railway had come this way, forging its route to Bristol and the West. Did you select your cricket membership and your railway carriage on the same basis?

As I crossed the Wiltshire border I came to Purton where cricket has been played since 1820. Purton players were selected to join those from Hungerford to play William Clarke's travelling All-England XI in 1852. One of Purton's players at that time was E. H. Budd, whose playing career had begun at Lord's at the turn of the nineteenth century. Budd was one of the best cricketers of the pre-Grace era who had taken part in the great single-wicket contests of the day. Purton were lucky to have Budd on their side in his old age and unlucky to have a star of a later era playing against them when the young W. R. Hammond trounced their bowlers in 1920 before being bowled 'with the aid of a plantain'. It was described to me as 'a place where visitors are always welcome, where good cricket is appreciated and where many people work selflessly for the good name of the club.'

Wiltshire villages give way to none in the charm of their names. With some sadness I passed by the cricketers of Compton Chamberlayne, Little Durnford and Kingston Langley and joined the M5 south of Bristol. Soon after entering Somerset, the motorway goes over the very ground of Ruishton Cricket Club which had fallen victim to the planners in 1975. But a club with a sixty-year history recovered from that tragedy. 'We found a local school to play at,' said Brian Jones, the secretary, 'and we're still among the leading villages in Somerset League

'I don't think we've played you before, have we? This is the first year we've played beyond Evercreech or Batcombe' (*Cartoon by Hargreaves*)

Cricket. Earlier this year we won the county knock-out final, with the scores level and fewer wickets down, against Coalpit Heath.'

The Ruishton cricketers had travelled that afternoon to Barrington to play a Somerset League match. There most of them had some feelings of envy as the team without a real home of their own met one which might claim with some justification to play on one of the prettiest grounds in England. As Ruishton's Bob Gray and John Cooling came out to bat I looked around. Beside the thatched wooden pavilion were garden shrubs backed by beech trees. Masses of oaks lined the field square to the wicket, while parkland lay beyond. An Elizabethan wall, below which flowed a gentle stream, was the only sign of man's habitation. Behind that wall, just out of sight, stood Barrington Court, a gracious Tudor mansion. Geese were among the spectators, and ivy grew up the shafts of the old horse-drawn roller which stood beside its modern successor. In such a setting may cricket be played in the Elysian Fields.

The scenery was possibly too much for Ruishton's batsmen who, earlier in the season, had comfortably beaten Barrington on their own borrowed ground. Wickets were falling fast until Peter Barrington took the bowling of his namesake team to task. But Ruishton's 80 would not be enough, Brian Jones ruefully told me as I slipped off to make my way to Evercreech. Ruishton's taunting motorway seemed light-years away as I meandered through remote lanes, passing two pre-war yellow-enamelled circular AA village signs, the kind we took down to stop German agents from knowing where they were.

Evercreech was a salutary reminder that cricketers cannot for long be detached from reality. The cricket ground was flanked by a large factory producing cheese and butter 'with plenty to put on your bread'. When a cold store was built beside the factory it removed what little scenic attraction the ground had.

I watched with particular interest Ian Neville, the opening bowler, take off his sweater as he began a spell after the tea interval. He had made it himself. Of all the occupations of village cricketers, his must be among the most unusual for he runs a cottage industry making cricket sweaters. The Evercreech men in the field, in their sweaters trimmed with red and green, looked a good advertisement for business.

The business of cricket was serious too, I noted, as Rodney Chinnock, Evercreech's leading batsman, set about chasing runs. 'Anyone who wants a game gets his chance on Sundays,' Ian Woodborne, the umpire had told me, 'we can put out a Sunday side with an average age of eighteen and beat a full men's team.' It was a view confirmed by a spectator: 'Evercreech has been one of the best village sides in the 1970s, but the emphasis now is on the young rather than immediate success.' I watched a sixteen-year-old batting well and agreed that village cricket in Somerset had a good future.

With Somerset cricket being played at places with names like Buckland St Mary, Chilton Crickets, Chew Magna and Leigh on Mendip it could hardly fail to make an appeal. In the days long before leagues and world wars you could play a Whit-Monday match at Beckington and have a home-cooked lunch and tea, or watch the sports and fête at East Chinnock going on alongside the game, or simply support the cause at Stoke St Mary by buying a whist drive ticket for 2s.

No doubt you could have done much the same in little Devon villages such as Clyst St George, Bishopsteignton or Chagford where life centred round small communities and where a Devon man, a hundred years ago, might visit Exeter once in a lifetime.

Far west in that county I came to the valley of the Lyd and the village of Coryton, where once they mined and still they farm, with a tiny cricket ground little distinguishable from the surrounding fields. The fathers and grandfathers of the men casually practising one Friday evening had gone far afield in two world wars, as the church war memorial recorded, to fight in France, Mesopotamia and North Africa. Nor had the village itself always been at peace. Not much more than a hundred years ago, the church clerk had been stag-hunted through the parish, for kissing a maiden in the choir. He married the lady and one of their descendants would play for Coryton next day against Brentor, the neighbouring parish three miles to the south; but no easy journey before cars brought everyone together for this, the local 'derby'.

If you came from Coryton you climbed several hundred feet out of the Lyd valley through narrow wooded lanes, setting your sights by the Brent-tor rising 1,100 feet above sea-level, on which was set one of the highest (and smallest) parish churches in England. St Michael's, Brentor, was built in the twelfth century, possibly as a thank-offering by some merchant who survived a shipwreck. For hundreds of years it 'serveth as a mark for sailors, who bear with Plymouth haven' wrote Tristram Risdon in 1625.

Once the Coryton cricketers reached the tor, their course lay a few hundred yards east to the cricket ground. Few grounds can need a sight-screen less, surrounded by the soft, unchanging contours of Dartmoor, with mile upon mile of folded hills. Those who bowl at the Brentor end have the tor with the church on top behind

No sight-screen is necessary at Brentor where the church on the tor presides over the cricket

them inviting batsmen to drive the ball impossible distances and to reach heights of fantasy.

Cricket at Brentor has had its ups and downs. For a period in the 1960s sheep grazed contentedly as no cricketers disturbed their pastures. Then came change. The game returned there in the 1970s because of the unlikely combination of a retired Eton schoolmaster and his Californian wife. Laurence Lefèvre brought something from the playing fields of Eton to Brentor. As chairman, secretary and umpire he is the ''Pooh-bah' of the village cricket. Everyone said so, and no one minded the 'foreigner' taking over.

When I watched that Saturday league fixture with Coryton, a trim field, closely mown to the boundary, met me with flag flying beneath a weather vane depicting a batsman—made by the village blacksmith—and a smartly painted green and white pavilion. Steve Cryer, Brentor's captain, was setting his field.

Joe Perkins—a good Coryton name—opened for the visitors, but was soon back in the pavilion ready to recall that Coryton's cricket wouldn't have been anything if it hadn't been for Farmer Trant. 'He gave us the field. We'd cut a strip and clear the cattle out before the game. We'd cycle up to play Brentor,' he recalled, 'take us all morning to get up the hill, then we got a van to take us.' 'Brentor had a cattle truck,' Frank Doidge added, 'used it for the cows Monday to Friday, and cleaned it out on Saturday morning for the cricket.' There were three Doidges playing besides Frank, who had been treasurer in the 1920s. In those days the players paid 4d a week all through the year and nothing else—no match fee, and a free tea. In the winter the money would be paid in the reading room. 'But we never bought the kit. You went into Tavistock and ordered bats and pads and put them down on the colonel's account. He was a rich man, worth a quarter of a million. The vice-presidents gave you thirty bob a year.'

By now six Coryton wickets were down for 56. Coryton were half-way up—or half-way down—the league with few matches left. Brentor were second top: the four points for a win, and the bonus for dismissing the opposition were vital. 'We don't get paid, you know,' Joe Perkins commented as his son Graham was bowled, playing indecisively to a well-pitched ball on the off-stump. Neither side dealt in high finance. Three pounds a season from the players and no match fee, plus an occasional barn dance, saw Coryton through the year, while Brentor got by on wine and cheese parties and £40 profit on the teas.

Tea was a grand occasion with the sort of cream, cakes and scones which breed plump Devon lads and lassies. The home team, with only 65 to win, could afford to enjoy it. Coryton would only be in the field an hour or two. No one quite knew whether Coryton's centurion (three this season) was absent through injury or silaging. The cricket seemed less important than it had in Somerset. 'We're out to relax on a Saturday afternoon,' said Roger Peek.

The church on the tor looked down on a pleasant setting of picnickers and players. Too soon, Brentor got the runs, and an hour of good cricket weather (in a wet summer) was wasted. Farmer, farrier, slaughterer, national park warden and all the Doidges, trudged into the pavilion, the former Eton master in his straw hat and umpire's coat carrying in the stumps and checking on next week's side. A notice in the pavilion caught my eye. 'The subscription in 1979 is reduced from £4 to £2.' Was the announcement unique in these inflationary days? Had the Eton mathematician played another trump card for the village that challenged the top of the league?

Presently people made their way to the pub. The Brentor Inn echoed to rich Devon voices discussing weather and fishing, market prices and farming, holiday-makers and caravanning. Frank Doidge thought I should have some more information. 'There's no cricket any more in Chillaton, Mary Tavy or Peter Tavy,' he said. 'They only played a lot when the mines were in full swing.' Not everyone agreed with that opinion. Perhaps only the church on the tor knew the answer. There it stood, picked out in the moonlight, pointing foursquare to all those little villages in the valley.

Sometimes village cricket flourishes where there is scarcely any evidence of a village any more. Such a place was Werrington where the nephew of that great Devon bowler, Sir Francis Drake, is remembered in a tablet in St Martin's church.

A Larry cartoon from *Punch*

'This is their best bat coming in, he once watched Don Bradman at the East Banford charity match—on a Thursday I think it was . . .' (*Cartoon by Hargreaves*)

The church itself, with stocks still standing outside to punish errant villagers or fielders who drop catches, looks towards the cricket ground on the Devon-Cornish border.

Cricket has been played at Werrington for more than sixty years on land belonging to Werrington Park, a dairy and sheep-farming estate of several thousand acres. In earlier days agricultural workers who lived nearby made up the team, but the community has moved away. Players come from other villages and from nearby Launceston to play for a side which won the Devon village championship in 1976 and 1977.

When they played against Troon, the Cornish village champions, they had a gate of over a thousand and took £500. 'We didn't do teas for that number so most people brought their own, but we served splits—bread with jam and cream,' the ladies told me.

That evening Werrington were fulfilling a fixture against the small village of Lewannick in the Launceston evening League. The gate was hardly a thousand and the secretary, Gordon Walters, had time to relax and talk.

'We've got a steady side, men who can make thirty or forty, no one spectacular, and no one who has ever played for the county, but plenty of youngsters coming on in the under-14 and under-13 sides. We've got to encourage everyone to buy their own kit. The 1st XI does already.' Werrington was a curiosity, a village so tiny that one looked in vain for much habitation, yet one of the very best village sides in the far west of England. Before I left Devon, I was told the story of the old lady whose son had joined a newly formed village club near Exeter. 'He's gone to play weasel,' she said. Mystified, her friends suggested it might be cricket which he had gone to play. 'Well, perhaps it were: 'twas some animal.'

Fortified by this tale I crossed the Tamar into historic tin-mining countryside. Here, in the east of Cornwall, is Callington. They were playing the tiny village of Gerrans, whose cricketers had made their way up through busy holiday traffic from the south of Cornwall to fulfil a fixture in Division I of the Senior Cornish League (East). That they had never beaten Callington seemed not at all surprising to the observer—little village pitted against small town. But I was reminded that this had little real significance in Cornish cricket. The East League included towns such as St Austell and Liskeard and villages such as Grampound and Veryan—and both these villages had beaten Callington that season.

Gerrans won the toss and chose to bat, happy enough to relax after sixty miles of almost bumper-to-bumper driving. Their opening bat, Bruce Nicholls, was a former county player. But the man they were proudest of was M. J. Harris, 'spotted by a holidaymaker at Gerrans and recommended to Lord's.' Harris had packed his Cornish bags as soon as he left school and had graced Middlesex cricket before he moved to Nottinghamshire for a number of years. 'Brings the Notts side down to Gerrans,' I was told.

Gerrans were second bottom of the league playing the runners-up. 'We need 180 on this ground, and we won't get them,' a player commented. After twelve overs, the total was 15 for two. The target seemed unlikely in a limited-overs game. The medium-pace bowling of Peter Moores, the Callington secretary and ground manager, and George Wyatt was good defensive stuff. Gerrans would later counter with an unusual attack, Bill Palmer and Horace Hedges, both slow orthodox left-arm bowlers used with confidence and success, even on their own tiny Gerrans ground.

Lower down the Gerrans' batting order was Poskus. No other name looked remotely Cornish, nor indeed was that of John Poskus—the only Lithuanian fast bowler playing in Cornish cricket. 'Come to Gerrans some time,' he told me, 'Best cricket tea in the county.' At 20 pence it sounds a bargain and with a match-fee of a further 20 pence, Gerrans cricketers were living as cheaply as any club I met.

In the Callington club-house, full of pictures of old teams, teas were being prepared by Marie Hand from Loch Lomond. 'I give them jam and cream tufts and salad for tea,' she said. She was also bar manager. 'I took the job on because they told me it meant serving a few pints on a Saturday afternoon and going home.' She paused. 'It doesn't.' Marie was there for every one of the seventy home games. Her bar made an annual profit of £500 and took her up to sixteen hours a week to run.

Marie's bar was called the Sobers Bar, in commemoration of when a very distinguished eleven led by Sir Garfield Sobers had played Callington. Cricketers do not think of international stars playing against Cornish clubs. Many supporters of the game would draw a vague line somewhere south-west of Gloucestershire and Somerset and conclude that cricket did not prosper beyond it. So I posed a question to which I would later return: 'Why was cricket so popular in Cornwall?' 'There's not a lot else to do in small places. The villages are closed communities. Down by St Mawes in the St Anthony-in-Roseland peninsula you've got six clubs within two square miles, some of them running two teams.' And everyone felt he was in with a chance to play for Cornwall. Elsewhere, most minor county sides were drawn from the players within a few strong town clubs. Young players of ability would be tempted away from village sides, and even less fashionable town ones, to play for the clubs which 'mattered'. 'But in Cornwall,' remarked a Callington player, 'if you're in the village side and you're good enough for Cornwall, you're in.' Then there are the leagues. All the teams are in the leagues—Cornish Senior East and West and Cornish Junior East and West, with their divisions. Towns and villages are all mixed up.

Among the more unlikely contributors to the success of Cornish cricket had been the former Liberal politician, Isaac Foot—famous radical thinker and activist, and

Callington, like many another Cornish side, have a long tradition of league cricket; here is their 1907 side

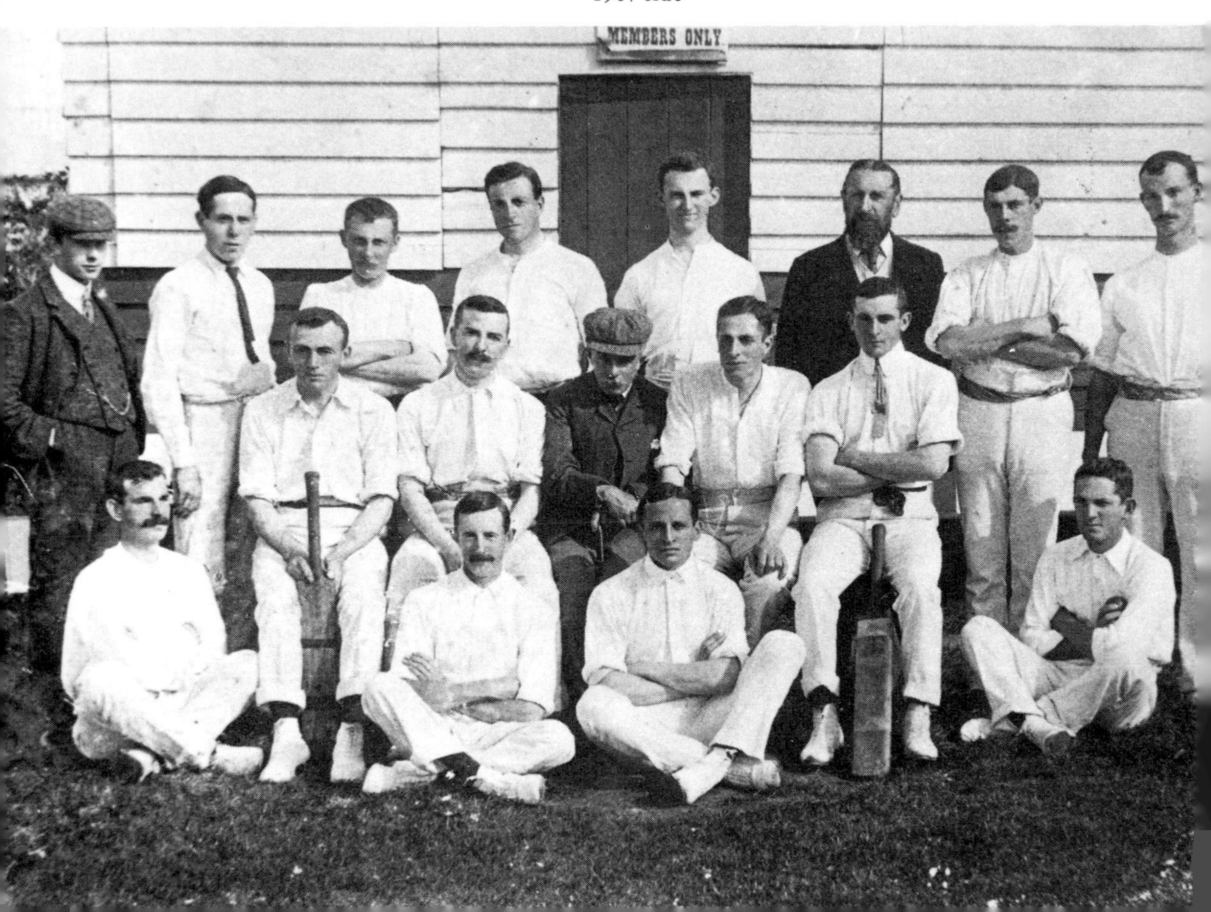

The Cornish side of the Tamar: Werrington v Gerrans; far behind the bowler's arm lies Brentor, as seen on page 77

father of three distinguished sons who made their careers in politics, diplomacy and the bar. Isaac Foot had established the evening village competition which bore his name, and which, in 1978, celebrated its fiftieth anniversary. All villages within ten miles of Callington (including some in Devon) might compete. In the 1978 final Tideford, south of Liskeard, beat Lifton, from just across the border in Devon.

Gerrans drove back that evening along empty roads. The south-bound holiday-makers were all safely tucked up in their caravans and guest houses. West of this route lay the forbidding expanse of Bodmin Moor, east of it lay familiar names and familiar cricket grounds—Looe, St Blazey, Tregony, St Goran. They still had to beat Callington.

I had one more port of call westwards. I had to find out why Troon, at the very foot of Cornwall, had been champion village in the British Isles on three occasions. The answer is in Chapter 8. My mission completed, I drove back north-eastwards, lingering for an hour to watch Werrington play Gerrans, and then made my way through Devon and Somerset to Gloucestershire.

Gloucestershire is in the county of the Graces, and the association of that most famous of all cricketing families with a group of villages north of Bristol has an interest of its own in village cricket folklore. Visit Downend, Thornbury, Frenchay and Stapleton and you will still find cricketers there ready to tell you about the Graces who played for them!

Go first to Downend where Henry Mills Grace was in practice as the local doctor. Despite not having an hour he could call his own he believed it was important to play with his children. Far removed from the typical remote Victorian father, he took time by the forelock and laid a cricket pitch in front of his house. There his five sons learned their early cricket. William Gilbert, the most famous of them, has related his memories of walking out of the front door to play cricket, 'as naturally as any other boy in England went into his nursery to play'. Soon Henry Mills Grace was persuaded to do for Downend what he had done for his own family. A village cricket club ground was prepared, and a club was formed which has flourished ever since.

Go, next, a few miles to Frenchay. You will see the common close by the parish church where all five Grace brothers played from time to time. Their mother, Martha, loved to watch her cricket on the common. She has her own place in cricket history. One can only conjecture how the game might have been affected if there had never been a W.G. Her eccentric father once suspended her from a kite to fly across the Avon Gorge! Frenchay still play their cricket but no longer on the old common.

Your journey from Frenchay to Thornbury, alas, will be scarcely rural any more as you pursue a network of motorway intersections to come to Thornbury's little ground beside the old Ship Inn. The pavilion is full of records of the Graces. Derek Hawkins, himself an old Gloucestershire player, has the enviable life of

The Grace family team in 1867: W. G. is on the left in a white cap, E.M. is in glasses in the middle and their father, H.M., is wearing a top hat

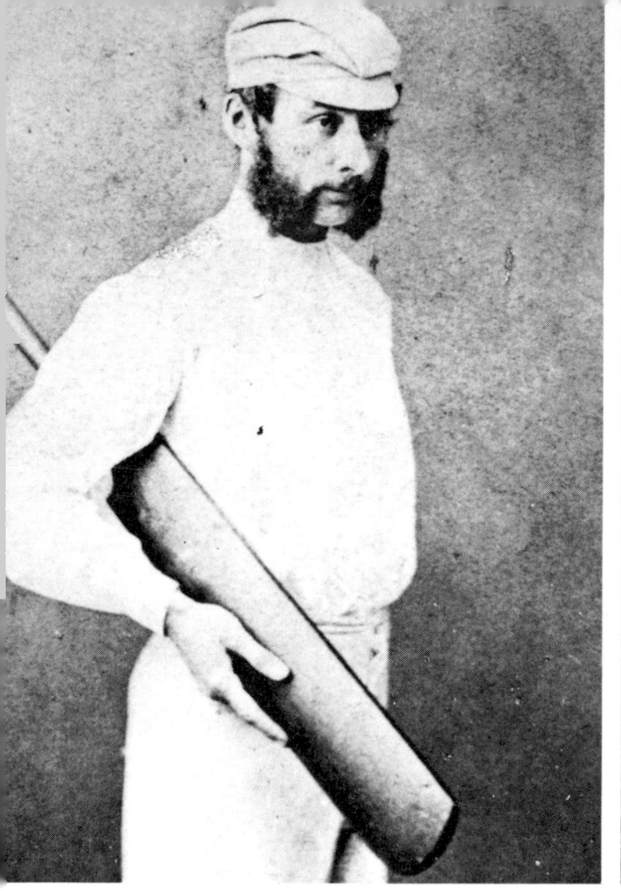

(*left*) E. M. Grace senior who made sixty-seven centuries for Thornbury (*MCC*);
(*right*) W.G.: a characteristic photograph of him bowling (*MCC*)

working in the family motor business which borders the ground and of playing for the club. He claims with justification that: 'Thornbury has the closest association with the Graces.' There can be no dispute. The club was founded in 1871 by Edward Mills Grace, W.G's eldest brother, who was its first captain, secretary and treasurer. His son, Edgar Mervyn, was to hold the same offices as well as becoming president. These two Graces served Thornbury in an unbroken link from 1871 until 1974. Edgar made his debut for the village at the age of nine, in 1895, and took six wickets for 24 with high-pitched lobs. In his fiftieth playing year he scored a century in a hundred minutes. He finally retired in 1957 after a playing career of sixty-two years. His cricket days spanned a period from the Jameson Raid in South Africa to the Suez crisis; from Gladstone to Macmillan. Edgar's son, Gerald, was still turning out occasionally in 1978, and a son in the fifth generation was born during that season.

W.G. himself played rather less for Thornbury, but there exists a score-sheet beside which nearly all other village innings must be put in the shade. One early

Dr. W. G. Grace
Had hair all over his face.
Lord! how the people cheered
When a ball got lost in his beard!

A cartoon by Nicolas Bentley

April day in 1881 the brothers W.G. and E.M., with some mild assistance from John Cranston, scattered the luckless opposition bowlers:

E. M. Grace c Hall b Eyles	228
J. H. King b E. King	56
S. Day b Hall	3
W. G. Grace Not out	196
J. Cranston Not out	174
Extras	17
Total (3 wickets)	674

Finally, make your way southwards again to the outskirts of Bristol where you will come to Stapleton. 'We are still a village, you know,' Wilfred Henley assured me. He had lived there all his life and had seen W.G. I had come that particular day by train and bus to watch Stapleton play at home. The afternoon was hot and sleepy and I was glad to turn off the Stapleton Road (where W.G. had once had his surgery) and enter the small rectangular ground with stumps of old diseased elms flanking one side. Some silver birches were beginning to take their place, not yet thick or tall enough to hide the stone Georgian house, The Elms, which lay alongside. At the top end of the field rose the gorseland of Purdown Hill. A fine oak tree stood beside the sight-screen.

Stapleton's claims are both ancient and modern. Their pavilion pictures testified to their feat in producing four players who represented England in the last generation: Jack Crapp, Arthur Milton, David Smith and David Allen. Allen, indeed, was selected for the village and for England in the same season.

'They're not our only Test players, you know,' they told me. 'W.G. played for us.' There it was, set out in the club rules for 1866: 'Captain, W. G. Grace: the captain be chosen for one year.' I read on: 'The eleven chosen to play in a match to appear in white flannel trousers.'

They came out to field, while I was reading, in their white flannel trousers. I settled down in a deck chair. It was getting hotter and the temptation to doze off was hard to resist. A wooden pavilion, which I hadn't noticed before, caught my eye and out of it emerged the opening batsmen, two bewhiskered men, the taller one remarkably young, wearing brown boots, and striding to the wicket with an air of great confidence. I thought I caught the strains of a rather high-pitched voice as he asked the umpire for his guard. The younger man threw his weight on his right leg and batted with the minimum of back-lift. Runs came steadily for the first half an hour or so as people began to come into the ground. There was some fuss as a barouche and pair of horses with a postillion turned up. An elderly clergyman arrived in a gig and there were several pony traps. A notice caught my eye: 'Admission 3d. If W. G. Grace plays 6d.' Well! W.G. *was* playing and I supposed I'd paid my 6d.

During the lunch interval the players walked past the line of tall elms to eat at the Georgian house. Someone told me there was a bottle of hock and salmon from the Severn. 'Rather grand,' I thought, until they said that the opposition were gentlemen who had come down from Swindon for the day. 'Thanks to Mr Brunel,' I murmured as I got myself a glass of ale and a sandwich for 7d. I could have sworn I'd already had lunch anyway that day.

'Howzat!'

A cartoon by Nicolas Bentley

When play was resumed W.G's partner, his brother E.M., seemed anxious to score quickly. Time and again he lofted the ball over the bowler's head towards the oak tree while W.G. drove more firmly along the ground, often square cutting to the wall on the short side. At 164, E.M. was the first to go trying to pull a ball outside the off-stump over mid-wicket. He had made a very creditable 66 and his brother was by then in the 90s. A cut past point saw W.G. to his century and shortly afterwards Mr Campbell very worthily claimed his wicket. It had been a capital innings. His departure gave heart to the Swindon bowlers. Some wonderfully accurate work from Mr Barrett dismissed the rest of the Stapleton side rather quickly, leaving his team 225 to win. Swindon, I fear, proved a weak opposition as E.M. bowling his lobs, took six for 50 and W.G. two for 15.

After the game tea was brewed in a large boiler and I was asked into the wooden pavilion. We ate cakes, buns, and warm bracks which were a sort of currant cake I hadn't met before. The Swindon team seemed a little disconsolate as I shared their horse-brake back to the Great Western Railway Station at Bristol. Our ways parted: the Swindon men caught the Paddington express. My high-speed diesel left from another platform. When I looked round to wave goodbye they had gone. Only the great Victorian arch of Bristol Temple Meads remained to give reality to my dream.

6
NINETEENTH-CENTURY VILLAGE

The Reverend Albert Barff, newly appointed to the vicarage of North Moreton, wrote in his diary one September evening in 1858: 'I have formed a cricket club. The farmers took this up warmly and, with myself, bore the expense of bats, stumps and balls. On the whole it has worked well.' A few days later he wrote that it gave him an area of influence in the parish and 'an opportunity to control drinking and bad language.'

Before the summer was over, three matches had been played against other villages and the season ended with a grand village occasion which set the tone of Barff's work in North Moreton. The Bishop of Oxford, Samuel Wilberforce, came to re-open the church. The village street was 'decorated with arches' and there was a cricket match in the afternoon followed by a supper in the tithe barn with 'soup and cold meat for all'. Barff called the day 'a turning-point in the life of the village.'

For centuries the natural boundaries created by an arc of the Thames in the north and by marsh-land in the south had given the small Berkshire* community of North Moreton a certain isolation. Oxford was a distant prospect, Didcot just another village, and Wallingford a key river point in the medieval monarch's control of the south of England.

The agrarian and industrial revolutions made significant, if undramatic, changes in the life of the village. By 1844 Brunel's railway from Paddington to the west passed just south of the village boundary and Didcot had begun to be an important junction. While the majority of men were labourers on the farms, a few sought work on the Great Western line as 'navvies', porters or signalmen.

Of more direct effect on North Moreton than the advent of the railways was the arrival of Albert Barff as vicar. Barff had been an undergraduate at Oxford during the religious fervour of the 1840s and he brought to North Moreton all the energy and commitment which the Oxford Movement had inspired. He came to a village composed entirely of farmers, labourers and those who supplied their needs. There was one baker, one horse dealer, one cooper and one travelling musician. Since the beginning of the century there had been an unvaried pattern of about 120 births per decade—or one a month.

*The village was transferred to Oxfordshire in 1974.

Albert Barff (in top hat) and some fellow-clergy in the early days of Moreton cricket; the man on his right may be putting his pads on!

North Moreton now found itself with a resident parson in the vicarage who set to work to repair the fabric of the medieval church, to institute a pattern of church worship along Tractarian lines, to establish a village school and, most of all, to ensure that the life of the villagers revolved around the vicarage. Victorian paternalism enveloped North Moreton under Albert Barff!

The linking of church functions with cricket matches was to prove a major feature of Barff's incumbency. In 1861, for example, the harvest festival programme included a service at 11 o'clock and a cricket match at noon. There was a tea at 5 o'clock for players and spectators alike. Then all attended an evening service with sermon at 7 o'clock. Afterwards there was a 'supper served in the schoolroom' with toasts to 'the farmer, the cricket club and the vicar'. For those who had any stamina left—remember that there had been two church services, a cricket match and two meals—a concert followed at which 'the choir and the ringers gave their services gratuitously.'

So ended a day 'whose most gratifying features,' the vicar noted, 'had been the genuine enjoyment of all, without the least excess; and the hearty unanimity and co-operation of all classes within the parish.'

Barff was always concerned about the conduct of his flock. A cricket match against Long Wittenham passed off with the 'behaviour of all being satisfactory'. Another game at Michaelmas, preceded by a service and followed by a cold meat supper, found everyone 'conducting themselves properly'. But an away fixture in Oxford to which the cricket club had gone with him by train proved too much for some. 'These men got away from me,' Barff recorded. There was excessive drinking and they had to find their own way back to Didcot station. 'It must not happen again,' Barff's notes concluded.

The vicar was keenly conscious of the Victorian evil of drink, although unlike his successor, not a total abstinence advocate. In a generous mood in July 1870, he provided the beer two weeks' running. On the first occasion, eleven married men played eleven single men in the village, the latter winning by 100 runs. The players contributed a shilling each to the dinner which followed. 'At 10 o'clock I broke up the party,' Barff wrote, 'for men had to be at work in the field and on the railway very early the next morning.' The second 'beer' match was an all-day game against neighbouring Cholsey in which twenty-seven wickets fell for 246 runs; the North Moreton curate, Mr Simeon, was top scorer with 25 and took five wickets.

Barff, like many Victorian incumbents, lived in the vicarage in some style. He resided in a village lacking a squire, so that the parson was the major social figure. A hint of the size of his household may be seen in his raising a cricket eleven 'from those dependent on the vicarage for employment', to play the Rest. It was a low-scoring game in which twenty wickets fell for 107 runs, the Rest losing by the odd run. Other tastes were catered for on that July day in 1871. Those who were neither playing cricket nor watching it might listen to a band in the vicarage garden to which (rather surprisingly) Barff charged an admission of a penny or threepence. When the cricket match ended, 'the cricketers returned to the garden to join in the dancing.'

Barff's last summer in the parish, 1872, may be taken as a typical year in the life of the cricket club he had founded. The season began on a new ground, given by the kindness of the farmers. The opening match was a trial between members of the choir and the rest of the village. Between 1.45 and 6.30, thirty-two wickets fell for 98 runs, Mr Simeon the curate again dominating the proceedings with 34 runs.

Seven of the choir eleven which had been victorious, were selected for the Moreton side a week later to play against Keble College, Oxford in an all-day game. Alas! Mr Simeon failed them, with 0 and 1, and the club lost by an innings and 35 runs. Jackson's *Oxford Journal* attributed their defeat to the 'bowling of Mr Bacton, which was exceedingly fast,' and 'to missed chances in the field by Moreton.' 'Accidentals', a quaint word for 'extras', contributed 17 to Keble's

Arthur Winter, the Cambridge wicket-keeper who dispensed with a long-stop

score. The reporter was clearly sympathetic towards North Moreton. He reminded readers that Keble was one of the strongest college sides in Oxford and that Moreton was a club which 'sustained one, and only one, defeat last year.'

A week later, the village travelled by train from Didcot to Wantage to play King Alfred's Grammar School there. A three-wicket defeat at the hands of the school eleven left their friendly reporter little to say except that the match ended 'amid intense excitement'.

Victory came at last in a home match against Hagbourne. An opening stand of 38 suggested that the new Moreton wicket had some redeeming qualities. But the return match against the Grammar School brought the season's third defeat by two runs. Barff's notes on the game gave three good reasons for Wantage's victory: Moreton were a man short (hardly Wantage's fault!), Higginson of Wantage bowled grubs, and 'we had to contend against an insufficient umpire.' That evening several of the Moreton players sang in a village concert.

Concerts were a regular feature of village life. Barff had the habit of getting everyone to perform, so that the cricketers were as likely to be singing solos or duets as the visiting preacher, the farmers, undergraduates from Oxford or the wives of local clergy. Such celebrities as John Keble and Edward King, later a famous bishop of Lincoln, sang in the village schoolroom.

Brightwell, against whom the club had played its first-ever match back in 1858, provided the next opposition. Mr Simeon did not play so that the press could say, unabashedly, 'the working men of Moreton met the working men of Brightwell.' Brightwell were dismissed for 30, 'one of their eleven being so disheartened that he refused to play any longer and to the surprise of his own party, Moreton and the bystanders, walked off the ground.' He must have returned, for Brightwell batted with the same eleven men in their second innings, losing the match by an innings and 29 runs. An eleven raised by Mr G. E. Wells, and containing seven players of that name, played a drawn match against Moreton on the village ground.

No matches were played between the middle of July and the beginning of September because of harvesting. But the club then played a further half dozen matches, ending the season in mid-October. Victories against Cholsey and the better of a drawn match against the local town side, Wallingford United, preceded a final fixture between the Village and the Vicarage. The Vicarage eleven's win by two runs was attributed, wrote Barff, to their 'ability to lift the grounders better.' After the match, which ended at 5 pm, being October, there was a tea followed by a church service.

Barff's work in the Moretons had ended as it had begun, in bringing together

Captain (to very unsuccessful lob bowler): 'Oi be sorry to 'ave to take 'ee off, Garge, but I must let the vicar 'ave a go before the ball gets egg-shaped' (*Punch*)

A Match on *Thursday* the *8th* of *June* *between* *Lamborne* *&*

Vale of White Horse 1st Innings

Order of going in.	Striker.	How out.	Bowler.	Runs.	
1	T. George	c Barnes	Peirce	0	0
2	G. Butler	bowled	Barnes	1	1
3	J. Smith	bowled	Peirce	1	1
4	R. George	c D. Kennard	Barnes	0	0
5	J. L. Weller	bowled	Barnes	0	0
6	T. Whitfield	c Martin	Barnes	11	2
7	A. Philps	bowled	Peirce	0	0
8	J. Skurry	bowled	Barnes	111	3
9	R. Butler	bowled	Barnes	111	3
10	T. Thatcher	bowled	Barnes	11	2
11	F. Fortescue	not out		11	2
	Wide Balls				
	No Balls				
	Byes			111111	7
	Leg Byes			11	2
					23

Lamborne 1st Innings

Order of going in.	Striker.	How out.	Bowler.	Runs.	
1	J. Reading	bowled	Weller	11121	7
2	G. Tuson	bowled	T. George	1211211	9
3	G. Martin	run out		11	2
4	A. T. Bew	bowled	T. Whitfield	11221211231	17
5	J. Peirce	bowled	T. George	31221311111	18
6	D. Kennard	bowled	T. George	2222111121	15
7	A. Saxon	c R. George	T. Whitfield	232	7
8	C. B. Barnes	bowled	T. Whitfield	121	4
9	W. Willis	bowled	T. George	122	5
10	R. Harvey	not out			0
11	R. Kennard	bowled	Weller		0
	Wide Balls			11111	5
	No Balls				
	Byes			3111111	9
	Leg Byes			1	1
					99

18 65 at Lamborne
The Vale of White Horse

Vale of White Horse 2nd Innings

Order of going in.	Striker.	How out.	Bowler.	Runs.		Total.
	T. George	bowled	Peirce	131121	9	9
	G. Butler	l. b. w	Peirce	15	6	7
	R. George	run out		1	1	1
	F. Fortescue	bowled	Peirce	21	3	5
	T. Whitfield	bowled	Barnes	1	1	3
	T. Thatcher	c Willis	Barnes	0	0	2
	R. Butler	std Peirce	Barnes	1122121	10	13
	J. Smith	std Peirce	Barnes	112131	10	11
	A. Philps	run out		0	0	0
	J. L. Weller	bowled	Barnes	211	4	4
	J. Skurry	not out		0	0	3
	Wide Balls			11	2	2
	No Balls					
	Byes			31211112111	15	22
	Leg Byes			1	1	3
					62	85

the various aspects of village life. He left at the end of 1872 to become headmaster of the choir school at St Paul's Cathedral, London. He had given much to the village and his departure was deeply regretted. Among many presentations was one from the cricket club. In some ways, his fourteen years were the best ones in the nineteenth century for the villagers. Soon afterwards the agricultural depression caused a sharp drop in employment, which jobs on the railway only marginally eased. The young moved away. In the period between 1870 and 1914 the birthrate was half what it had been earlier. In the 1890s only forty-nine children were born in the village in ten years compared with one hundred and twenty-two in the 1860s. While eighty-eight marriages were performed between 1840 and 1860, only twenty-seven took place between 1880 and 1900. All this had its effect on the life of the community and the cricket club.

Barff's successor, the Reverend William Young, was to serve North Moreton from 1872 until his death in 1909. He continued the association between the vicarage and the cricket club and, unlike Barff, played himself. In May 1873, the first summer month of his incumbency, he turned out for the club and organised a 'Penny Reading' in the school to raise funds for it. He also continued Barff's custom of recording the main events of village life. Shortly after his arrival he brought a new and important recruit to the Moreton side in his curate, Arthur Winter, who had won a cricket 'Blue' at Cambridge.

Winter had been the first wicket-keeper in the university side to dispense with a long-stop. Subsequently, he had played a few games for Middlesex and for the Gentlemen. During his spell playing for Moreton the club benefited enormously from his batting and wicket-keeping.

Barff had established a fixture with St Edward's School, Oxford and an eleven played the village regularly until 1874 when the two sides met for the last time. Perhaps 'the fast underhand bowling of Lewis' had something to do with it, as St Edward's were dismissed for 7! More probably, the departure of Barff had weakened the connection between the small Berkshire village and the newly-founded Oxford school. Winter had played in the Moreton side, while the St Edward's eleven had included a boy called Russell Bencraft who got in the Hampshire side two years later, became county captain and was subsequently knighted. He was twice clean bowled by Lewis in that afternoon for 0 and 3! But the real celebrity of the match was the scorer, Kenneth Grahame, whose *Wind in the Willows* was based on Berkshire villages such as North Moreton.

After a gap of exactly 100 years, the fixture was resumed in 1974. The occasion was celebrated with an exhibition of old records and photographs. One Moreton member, Bud Finch (who, in his seventies, still plays an occasional game), was a

The St Edward's School, Oxford, side which played Moreton in 1872; Russell Bencraft is standing, holding bat, on the right

'The poor wickets . . . bedevilled standards . . .' (*MCC*)

living link with the match of a century earlier in that he could recall some of the village players as old men.

Under Barff a fixture-list had been created with the surrounding Oxfordshire and Berkshire villages, two or three schools and some Oxford colleges. Local town sides such as Wantage and Wallingford were also played. Scores tended to get higher as, no doubt, wickets improved, but a great many matches still allowed both sides to bat twice. The scoreboards of the day provided a column for totalling the two innings of each batsman. No manuscript score-book of Moreton survives but among their opponents were the Vale of the White Horse and Lambourn. The Vale club is no more but its old score-book survives with a reminder, on every page, that 'cricket bats, balls, stumps, chests and chains, with the Laws of Cricket, and new Scoring papers may be had of M. Dark and Sons, Bat Makers, at their Manufactory, Lord's Cricket Ground.'

Queen Victoria's Golden Jubilee in 1887 brought a full day of activities reminiscent of those which Barff had organised in his time. Proceedings began at 5.15 a.m. with a peal of bells in the fifteenth-century church tower. A service was followed by a number of parties given by the farmers. Then came *two* cricket matches. The married men played the single men (an old village 'hardy annual') and lost by one run. After a late tea, their feminine counterparts played a similar match. After the married women had been dismissed for 6, the single women batted on to reach 29 for six wickets. Play then ended for the day and a huge bonfire was lit beside the ground. Young's notes concluded: 'Everyone acknowledged that a happy pleasant day had been spent,' and added, 'though other places may have attempted more, we are convinced that Jubilee Day will not soon be forgotten in North Moreton.'

In 1888 Young deplored the condition of the cricket field, as 'ludicrously unfit

Reverend umpire (to village bowler): 'Now, my friend, how do you bowl? Round, or over, the wicket?' Bowler: 'Well, Zur, zometimes I bowls this way and zometimes t'other, but mostly I bowls at their legs!' (*Punch*)

The Moreton choir of eleven! 'Many must have played cricket because it was as much part of the natural scene as the church choir . . .'

for any but ''child's play''.' The poor wickets on which the club played had bedevilled standards through the entire century. Beyond occasional rolling and cutting, little was done to provide what could, in any sense, be designated a 'square'. Only once, before 1914, did a Moreton score top the 200, when they scored 219 against Hagbourne.

The Queen's Diamond Jubilee Day in 1897 followed similar lines to that of 1887. One significant feature was Young's decision to 'rejoice on total abstinence principles.' Employers of labour 'gave dinner to their employees and their families,' and the vicarage provided 'a high tea for all parishioners'. Between the two meals a cricket match was played.

Young was a stern advocate of temperance. He had founded a branch of the Temperance Society in the village as soon as he arrived and, at its first meeting, secured the 'pledge' from nine adults and seven children. He once publicly argued the case for bringing back the village stocks for drunkards and brewers alike. The publican who played in the cricket team, was designated by Young in the church registers as a 'keeper of a beer house'.

The Moreton village side in 1913

Playing a Canadian eleven 'sixty years on'; the author is keeping wicket and the 'home-grown Blue' is gully to the left-hander

From time to time both Barff and Young brought friends from outside—usually fellow-clergy—to play for the village, but on the whole the Moreton club was a side composed of those born and bred in the village. The same family names occur time and again in the score-sheets—Butcher, Cozens, Frank, Gregory, Mangin, Rowant, Saunders, Stickley, Shaylor, Slade, Wigley and Wing. None achieved fame on the field. Many must have played cricket because it was as much part of the natural scene as the church choir (in which they sang) and the clothing club (to which they contributed). As well as noting their cricket scores, Barff and Young had carefully recorded their attendances at choir and their contributions to the clothing club.

But such Victorian paternalism was soon to end—the first signs were evident in Young's time. For Moreton cricketers the era of their nineteenth-century club ended with the outbreak of war in 1914. A photograph shows them to be very much the same sort of people for whose grandfathers Albert Barff had founded the club two generations earlier. The vicar sits in the centre of the picture with one or two farmers in support. The players, on the whole, are the agricultural workers and the railway employees of a village community still remote, deferential and obscure. They would be surprised, indeed, to consider the thought that their small club, another sixty years on, would go away on tour, produce a home-grown university 'Blue' and entertain a visiting team from Canada.

7
SCOTTISH SPECTATOR

'Lambs have no road sense' was the solitary signpost on the lonely road across the Lammermuir Hills leading southwards to the village of Manderston, a few miles within the Scottish border. Down that road had tramped adventurers seeking their fortune and Jacobites supporting their prince. Up it had come the invading armies of Edward I, Henry VIII and Oliver Cromwell.

Highlanders from Luncarty had just journeyed down it from their home in Perthshire, for a first-round national village competition tie. They had come from a small village whose cricket has a functional look about it. There are no airs and graces about the Luncarty Club, which shares its ground and pavilion with footballers and whose cricket bows out sadly in the middle of August. The small community centres around the bleachworks, founded two centuries ago, and its cricketers are employed within the village. 'There are only fourteen cricketers in the club,' said Sam McGowan, secretary and all-rounder, 'there's a farm manager, a plumber, a joiner, a painter, a postman and an engineer. The others work in the factory.' 'We take our cricket seriously,' added Brian Ferguson, 'and we have to. There's no cricket in the schools and we teach the youngsters ourselves.'

They might be forgiven for envying the Lowlanders at Manderston their setting, where a captain could place his field by the variety of trees surrounding the ground with pines at third man and firs at fine-leg. 'Mid-wicket go to the elms, and cover by the pavilion yews,' he would announce, 'and mid-off and mid-on in front of the ash and lime.'

Luncarty came out to bat in this arboreal scene and found runs hard to get on a slow wicket. My attention wandered towards the fine stately mansion bordering the ground. 'Yes, there's always been support from there for our cricket,' commented David Luke. 'The family first made their money in trade with Russia in the last century. Then Sir James won the Derby. You can see the colours of his horse. They're the same as our club cap.' Fine-leg came out from the lee of the fir trees to save a Luncarty single, and display his vivid headgear. 'In those days the grooms and gardeners and butlers played for Manderston. They came from England to work on the estate. Nowadays we're mostly a team of farmers.'

Presently Luncarty passed the 100 and Jim McNichol got near to his 50. John Swan, bowling his off-cutters, looked the best of the Manderston attack. At 132 for eight, after the statutory forty overs, Luncarty closed their innings.

During a tea interval of magnificent proportions with cress sandwiches, rock cakes and scones, I learnt more about Manderston's past. For nearly forty years the ground had been cared for by the voluntary work of John Dawes, a Yorkshireman and head-groom on the estate. When the club secretary offered him an honorarium after many years of devoted service he tore up the cheque and it took everyone's tact to persuade him to continue in office.

The club had been founded in 1899 and survived a fixture in its opening weeks which might have caused many another institution to founder at birth. The opposition made 287 and dismissed Manderston for 33. Possibly discretion entered into the choice of fixtures, for the Minutes in 1900 recorded that 'fixtures with Kelso and Melrose were declined'.

The links with Manderston House have always been close, if somewhat unusual. The factor of the estate is still *ex-officio* president of the club while a Minute of 1902 noted that men employed in some building work on the mansion might not become actual members but would be allowed to play in two matches.

Manderston cricketers are proud of their past. They told me of Peter Wilson who took six wickets against Kent when the county toured Scotland in 1925 and who played against the New Zealanders two years later. On many occasions between the wars Wilson topped batting or bowling averages, sometimes being eclipsed by

'Let's have the cress sandwiches finer and deeper, and the rock cakes squarer . . .' (*Cartoon by Ray Chesterton from Heard in the Slips edited by R. Anderson, published by Stanley Paul & Co*)

'I was just saying to my son here, I can't see your lot getting all that many!' (*Cartoon by Ray Chesterton from* Heard in the Slips *edited by R. Anderson, published by Stanley Paul & Co*)

William Swan, Lord Lieutenant of the county and President of the Scottish Cricket Union, and as proud of Manderston hospitality as he was of its past. 'We had a lunch the other day,' he said, 'in which we offered chocolate ice cream and Christmas pudding—a hedge against any weather. And if you come in August, there's a match against the Cryptics when you'll find four or five kinds of cakes and as many varieties of scones.'

Teams such as the Cryptics, Oxford Authentics and Yorkshire Young Cricketers were among those who played at Manderston, while the club's fixture-card contained dates of the current Test matches and of all the finals at Lord's save the National Village final! Sadly their pessimism in that direction was not misplaced. Hopes of getting to Lord's crashed rapidly as David Patton and Jim McNichol of Luncarty trundled them out for 47. McNichol had had a good match. He needed to. He had run out of his three partners, including his captain, without facing a ball!

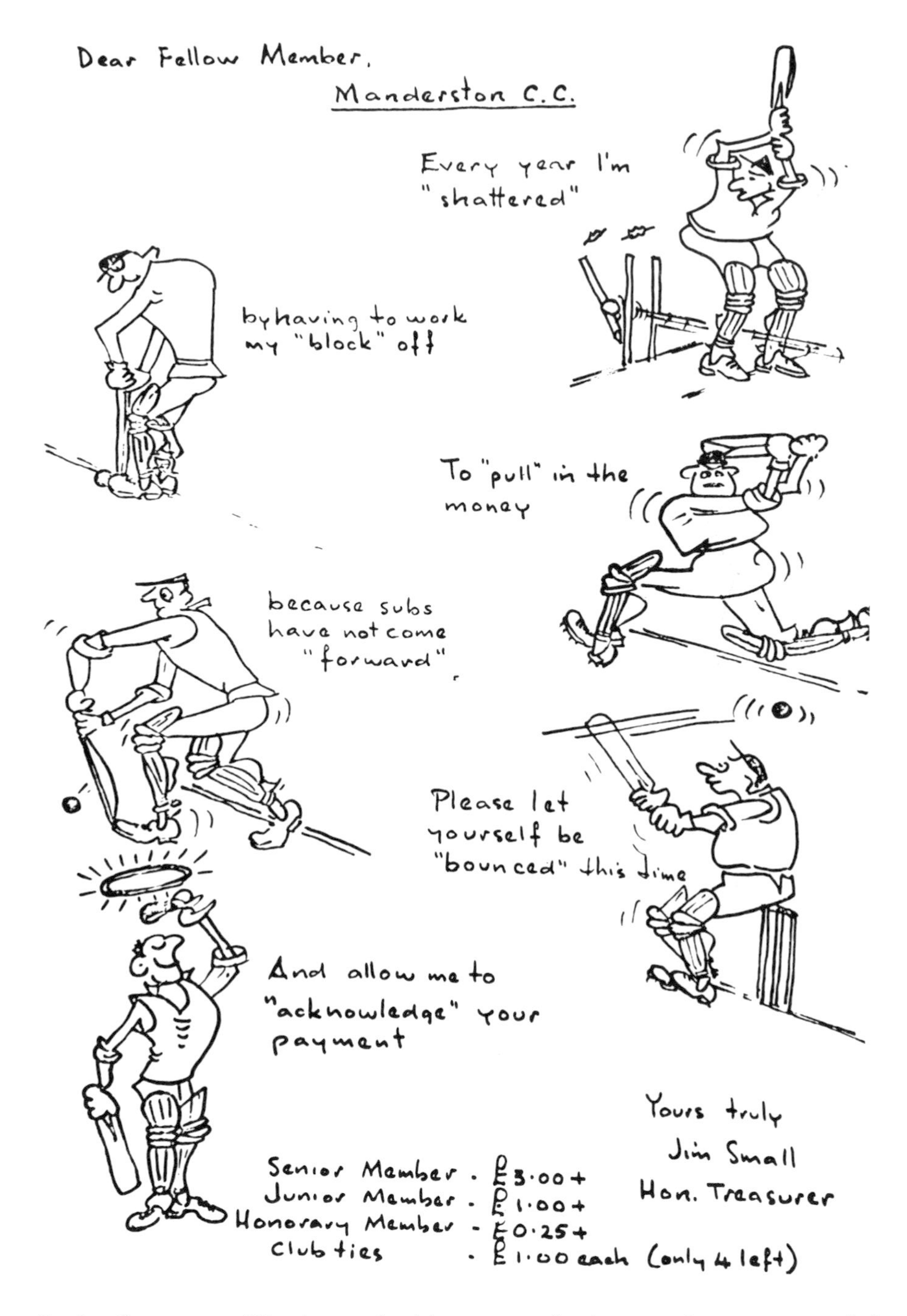

Jim Small, treasurer of Manderston, has his own ways of trying to get Scotsmen to pay their subscriptions

Luncarty, with a fine win behind them, drank Manderston's beer, and made their way north through the darkness of those lonely hills up to their Highland fastness. Their own prospects of taking the long road to England and Lord's were kept alive for some weeks as Glendelvine, Falkland Palace and Melrose fell victim to them. Sam McGowan did his best in the Scottish final at Scone Palace when he took seven for 13, but Luncarty fell for 36. The little club of fourteen members paying a subscription of £3 a year had no reason to feel dismayed.

I talked club finance with Manderston's treasurer, Jim Small, as he showed me the cartoons he drew to shame his players into paying. 'We have honorary members here,' he said, 'they pay twenty-five pence.' I remembered, of course, we were in Scotland.

Grooms and butlers from the south had helped create a cricketing tradition at Manderston. Not far away kennel-lads had brought the game to St Boswells where the Duke of Buccleuch's stables still stood beside the village ground. Successive dukes and their heirs (the earls of Dalkeith) have played for the club, as have the family of the earls of Home. A brother of the fourteenth earl had taken over 250 wickets for St Boswells, while the fourteenth earl himself (though no longer an earl but an ex-prime minister instead), had opened the new pavilion. Lord Home's cricketing credentials were strong. He had been president of the MCC and he had played for Middlesex.

St Boswells take pride in the club's records and statistics, in having two secretaries, W.E. and J. K. Ballantyne, between 1895 and 1977, in scoring 256 for two against the Eton Ramblers in 1950, in dismissing Hawick for 5 in 1928, in an earlier Lord Dalkeith who, with David McConnel, chased and passed Selkirk's 184 in less than two hours in 1935, in Alec Scott who had made over 15,000 runs for them and taken nearly 700 wickets.

Scott, a big burly man with forty years of village cricket behind him, was batting confidently against their local rivals Melrose. Peter Glover, with 6,000 runs to his credit for St Boswells, was supporting him well at the other end and David Nichol of Melrose was swinging the ball both ways.

St Boswells are equally willing to tell their visitors of their worst performances. The club noticeboard records that a certain S.D. appeared three times for the club in its history, scoring 4 runs. St Boswells also admit to being dismissed for 15 by Selkirk in 1908.

Presently Glover was back in the pavilion to tell me that 'Cricket in the borders is in a healthy state. A lot of it came up here when Englishmen moved north.' The manufacture of hosiery brought Yorkshiremen to Hawick in the 1830s. One of the early Hawick players would always field at long-stop. Legend has it that he was small and knock-kneed, and that he would drop on his knees every time he stopped the ball. The tweed industry had led to cricket at Gala in the 1850s, and paper-makers from the south took the game to Penicuik. Employees on the

St Boswells in 1895 when Lord Dalkeith was president and W. E. Ballantyne was secretary

Seventy years later when Lord Home opened the pavilion; J. K. Ballantyne, W.E.'s son, was secretary

Buccleuch estates had helped to start Langholm as well as St Boswells. Long before then, the English garrison 'red-coat' troops after the 1745 Jacobite Rebellion played cricket in Aberdeenshire, being reproved as 'scarlet vermin of hell' for so doing in a Cameronian pamphlet.

It wasn't always English influence which started cricket in Scottish villages. Brechin in the north had formed a 'society for the practice of this invigorating game,' because the local folk got tired of catching special trains to Montrose to watch cricket there. Who started cricket in Montrose? And what a delightful name had that club founded in the 1870s called Burnfoothill Brase of Doon Blossom—whose opponents included Burnfoothill, Heatherbell and the Vale of Doon and Dunaskin.

Clubs with more prosaic names such as Hawick, Gala and Melrose told me I was in Border rugby country. 'We produced C. W. Drummond,' Glover added. Presently the Melrose cricketers came in to tea and remarked that their club had been founded in 1894, had struggled between the wars, never winning the Border League, but had made a recovery in the 1950s largely due to an international rugby player J. L. Allan, who was still going strong after scoring nearly 8,000 runs for them.

'Go and see our ground on your way back to Edinburgh,' they said and I drove the few miles into Melrose. 'Wait now, I think you'll find it a mile or so up on your left,' explained the man at the petrol station beside the rugby ground. 'You've come too late for the spring sevens,' he added gratuitously. For Melrose is in the heart of Border rugby. Men with ambitions to play for the 1st XV eschew earthly pleasures as they train nightly below the great stadium. There was no stadium at the quiet little cricket ground without a house in sight. Only the mighty Eildon hills presided impartially over both sports.

Luncarty, which had beaten Manderston, was as far north as my Scottish travels took me. I had only just penetrated the Highlands, and Luncarty players told me of a match in the far north they had played against Fochabers in Morayshire one June which ended in snow. They had struggled southwards to reach home by 3 a.m. On another occasion they made a northern journey to Crathie where Sam McGowan had a field-day, taking four for 6 and making almost as many runs as the entire Crathie side on a ground within the private Balmoral estate.

Among Luncarty's opponents was Scone Palace to whom they lost in the Scottish Village final. Scone Palace was yet another example of a village club owing a great deal to the support of the Scots nobility. James Leven, an employee on the palace estate, described the sixth earl of Mansfield as 'a patron of father-figure proportions, whose enthusiasm was contagious in that it brought out the best in the members in every way, whether playing or in the running of the club.'

The sixth earl died in 1935 but the foundations were firmly laid. After the war Scone Palace opened its ranks both to estate workers and to residents of nearby

Cricket at Rossie Priory in 1879 and 1979

New Scone. The club entered Perthshire league cricket in 1968 and were league champions on four occasions in the next ten years. In 1978 they crowned these years of achievement by becoming the champion village in Scotland. Furthermore, four of the village side had appeared in the Perthshire county side while one was selected for the Scottish International XI.

Scone Palace cricketers play on a picturesque ground in front of the fine baronial mansion. As I passed out of the gates, I noticed the Mansfield family motto: *Spero Meliora.* To a club going through a lean spell, it might be loosely translated, 'One hopes for better things.' Scone Palace, on their 1978 form, had no need of such encouragement.

A late evening drive through the lovely Carse of Gowrie took me to Rossie Priory, one of the oldest centres of cricket in Scotland. I remembered playing there just after the war in front of the grand Scottish baronial-style house whose owners, the barons Kinnaird, have done so much to encourage the game. I bade farewell to the Highlands, crossed the Tay Road Bridge, passed Falkland Palace where there is a club under the lee of the Lomond Hills and came to Edinburgh. Clubs like the Grange and Carlton would be playing on the morrow but it was time to leave Scotland, the country where I had grown up and played cricket as a boy.

What is different about village cricket north of the border? The realist will say it is of a lower standard. The purist will point to the difference in wickets where batsmen usually have plenty of time for their strokes. The statistician will find few names known in the south to have come from these Scottish stables, though I. A. R. Peebles and M. H. Denness, both England Test-cricketers, have played the game locally. Let my own Scottish judgement be this: the village game reveals the people. It has a dour quality but it is not without warmth. Its players can be spartan when the elements demand. Their ladies provide scones a Sassenach would envy. Folk of all causes and circumstances blend easily within its ranks.

8
TWENTIETH-CENTURY VILLAGE

Ninety-year-old Steven Angove was watching the match against Camborne. He had first appeared for a Troon side against Truro at the turn of the century, and in between he had seen it all happen. Five-year-old Andrew Rashleigh was batting confidently in a quiet corner nearby. He would, they said, be well established in the Troon side—and probably the Cornish one as well—at the turn of the next century.

The old man remembered the journey to Truro. They made the twenty-mile trip in an open jersey-car drawn by four horses, and the working hours of those far-off days in 1908 only allowed them four hours for the actual match. Yet, over 400 runs were scored, Troon winning by the narrow margin of 4. He remembered Ronald Vibart's century and his liking for beer. He remembered his own last game for Troon: 'I gave up in 1925; I never got over the malaria I caught in Salonika.'

The pitting of the small tin-mining village against the growing cathedral city of Truro might seem an unfair contest but Steven thought otherwise. 'We felt equal to them, and to the other towns we played. Of course, we practised harder than they do today.' Some of those watching would have disagreed with him.

Troon, in entering the western division of the Cornish League in 1908, came up against opponents such as Truro, Falmouth, Redruth, Camborne, Penzance and St Just. Of them all, Camborne were seen as the special rivals because they were the nearest community. For the next forty years the village side flourished without ever winning the league championship. From time to time players such as Kit Trevarthen and Sam Hosking got capped for Cornwall, while Charles Rickard's county debut in 1933 saw him make 116 not out, largely off the bowling of a future England prospect, D. V. P. Wright.

Championship success came their way after the Second World War when Troon won the Western League in 1947 and then took on Gorran, the Eastern League winners. Rickard made 134 not out in Troon's score of 307 for two, supported by 92 from George Rogers, who had recently made 191 for the county against Dorset on the local Camborne ground. So good an eye had Rogers, it was said, that in his job as a linesman with the Electricity Board, he could set the posts up without any need to measure their positions. Gorran collapsed for 101, and Troon were the undisputed champions of all Cornwall.

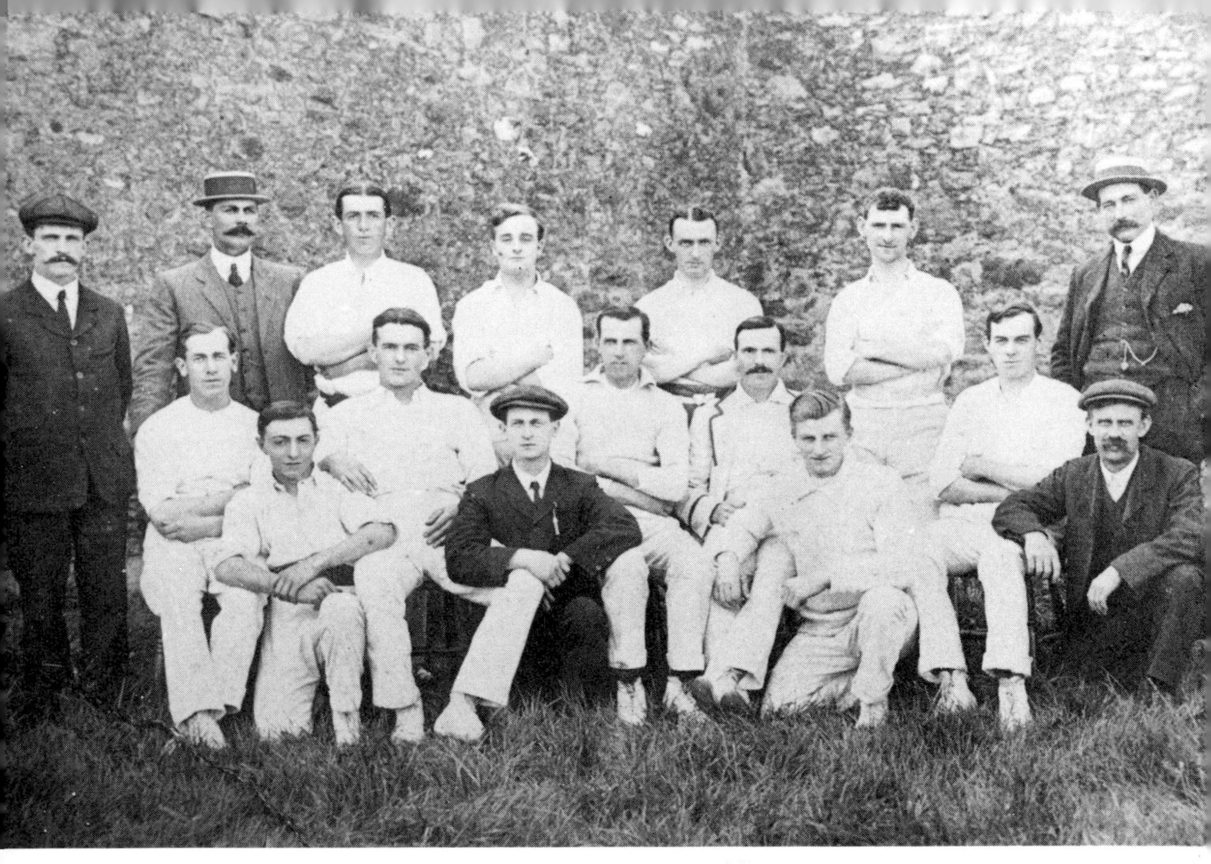

Troon in their early days in Cornish League cricket; Steven Angove is second from the right in the back row

That 1947 side was one of local men. The only player the club 'poached' was Fred Dingley, and it was not so much another team which suffered as his wife! Dingley was a schoolmaster down in Cornwall on holiday and he was urged by Troon's secretary, Maurice Bolitho, to play for Troon that August. He came back to play every August while his wife got to know the Cornish beaches.

As the side walked off the field after defeating Gorran, there were beaming smiles on the faces of older spectators such as Stephen Angove who had waited years for the triumph. The players felt that Troon cricket had come of age and that they, as individuals, had an important place in the life of the village community.

Exactly a quarter of a century later, in 1972, Troon became the best village cricket side in the British Isles with a display of proficiency which the sponsors of the national village competition had not expected and which the press admired. The question was inevitably asked: what is a village and what is a village cricket team?

Troon, with a population of under 2,000, was undoubtedly a village and her cricketers were home-grown. Troon-born men, whose fathers and grandfathers had played before them and whose sons would play after them, took the side to the summit of village cricket. And there lay part of the clue to success: men (and women) stay in Troon all their days.

Picture then, a small community of terraced houses built in local granite, projecting in four directions from the village square which has stood unchanged for a hundred years. There is a busy grocer's shop where the results of the away championship ties were received by telephone and whitewashed on to the shop window along with the week's bargain lines. Far into the night, cars would drive from the surrounding countryside, flash their lights on the shop window, and drive away. Cricket was good for business, as Walter Edwards, the grocer, freely admitted. There is a single public house, two Methodist chapels and an Anglican church. Children go to the primary school and thereafter to the comprehensive school in Camborne, two miles away. You can walk from end to end of Troon in fifteen minutes. To buy a new suit, change a library book, pay your rates, service your car and get your hair done would take you further afield.

Troon was built by a Victorian generation engaged in earning its living by extracting tin from the mines. The houses in the village reflect, in their simplicity and severity, the seriousness of purpose which has governed so much of Troon's

Andrew Rashleigh

history. Cricket was a leisure activity to be taken as earnestly as work. It was a man's business. Until recently no woman might participate in club functions.

On a working day the village streets are deserted save for old age pensioners and a few housewives. Jim Vincent, off work through injury, limped past, 'We'd have beaten the 1947 side,' said the veteran left-hand bat of the 1972 victorious village eleven. Only Maurice Bolitho was there to argue. 'We'd have had you all in trouble with our slow bowling.' 'Would Troon ever win again?' I asked Jim. 'It's something all the youngsters want to do. Get to Lord's. They're cricket crazy.' For the distant Cornish village with its strong Methodist tradition Lord's has become a Mecca for each generation.

Troon had known sharp adversity soon after the First World War. World tin prices dropped and the local mine closed. The mine still stood, its chimney stack somewhere at a distant third-man behind the cricket ground. It had shut down in 1922, just a few years before Steven Angove gave up playing. A deep depression hit Troon, so severe that children in London gave their pence to pay for a children's party in Troon. Men were flung out of work and the agony lasted for fourteen years.

Maurice Bolitho's father went to work in Wales and his older brothers joined a small Troon exodus to Detroit. Maurice was eight when it happened, lucky enough soon to win a grammar school scholarship and subsequently a university place. 'You'll never dirty your hands again,' commented his grandmother. Dirty hands or no, he remained a Troon man, playing cricket from the 1930s onwards and serving as secretary from the 1940s onwards. Cricket meant much to Troon in those depressed days. No one owned any kit but a club bag existed. Men on the dole played for hours on the field. On Saturdays they enjoyed a certain status. Clad in white, they challenged the towns of the Western League. Poverty was forgotten in achievement, destitution set aside by success. Cricket for some meant that sanity was preserved and dignity sustained. If you were unemployed, somehow the club found the money to pay your coach fare to the match at Truro. Sometimes you walked to the game in Redruth or Camborne.

In a way, Hitler was the unlikely source of revival in Troon's fortunes. As British politicians realised the need for re-armament instead of appeasement, airfields were built from which to attack a potential invader. By 1936, building them in south Cornwall absorbed the unemployed in Troon. A man could pay his match fee without embarrassing his wife's shopping money. After the Second World War, full employment was available. Men worked largely in the mining machinery firm of Holman Brothers. Soon, factories specialising in light industry grew up near the village while local service industries in Redruth and Camborne offered a third area of employment.

Whether in troubled times or in prosperity, most of the people of Troon have stayed in their home village and this has contributed to the remarkable continuity of family links in the village cricket club.

The decision of that club in 1972 to enter the national village cricket competition was taken lightly. 'We were just entering another competition,' commented Maurice Bolitho. But the real significance of the decision lay in the club's commitment to Sunday cricket—never before played in a strong non-conformist community. Some supporters were lost but an application to the grounds committee of the local Urban District Council to play cricket on the ground (which the club leased) was successful.

Little could the Troon players have realised the implications of their policy when they played the opening rounds against the villages of Boconnoc, Werrington, Gorran and Thorverton. The match against Thorverton, for the Devon and Cornwall title, was closely-run, owing most to a half-century from left-hander Tommy Edwards. Sixth and seventh round successes against Evercreech in Somerset and Shillingstone in Dorset brought Troon to the quarter-finals and an away draw against the Buckinghamshire side of Bledlow.

By this time Troon cricketers had come to face some of the stern realities of the competition. Between 7.30 on a Saturday evening, when a Cornish League match ended, and 7.30 on Monday morning, when work began for the majority of the side at Holman Brothers, a match had to be played at Bledlow and a round trip of nearly 700 miles taken.

The side set off by coach up the hundred miles of Cornwall, past the latecomers

The village comes to Lord's—for the first time; the Troon side in 1972

driving south in the usual Saturday haul of holiday-makers. Bed and breakfast had been fixed up in Exeter, and by 9.30 on the Sunday morning, Terry Carter, Troon's captain and a county rugby and cricket cap, had his men on the road eastwards.

A tired eleven found itself having to field against Bledlow, on the pretty ground nestling at the foot of the Chilterns. Gradually the hopes of a match at Lord's slipped away as Bledlow reached 100 for one and 150 for two. When the fortieth over was reached, Bledlow had set Troon a target of 205—five an over.

At 57 for four, Troon's defeat at the hands of the Royal Grammar School, High Wycombe, rather than at those of Bledlow seemed likely—a boy had made many of the Bledlow runs and a master had taken three of those wickets. And then skipper Terry Carter was joined by Jim Vincent—both established county players. Their partnership of 148 saw Troon home with eight overs to spare, Carter hitting eight sixes and ten fours. Even the 900 or so Bledlow supporters 'could scarce forbear to cheer,' said their secretary, John Samways, commenting that the match had done a great deal for cricket in the community.

All through Sunday night, the Troon side drove to the south-west reaching home in the early dawn—time for a shave before the work-hooters went.

A fortnight later it was the turn of Brian Carter, another Cornish cap, to share in a century partnership with the only man in the side not to come from Troon, John Spry. The pair were largely responsible for Troon's semi-final victory by nine wickets over Linton Park, the Kent side who were to be the 1978 champions.

By this time most cricket supporters in the British Isles were associating Troon with cricket rather than with golf. Certainly all Cornish roads led to Lord's on 9 September 1972, though sadly the railways did not. The specially-booked British Rail train broke down at Dawlish in Devon, leaving some 600 Troon supporters disappointed and angry.

Troon's opponents were the Warwickshire village of Astwood Bank, whom they put in to bat on a wicket damp from overnight rain. An opening stand of 69 and a third wicket stand of 70 were not enough to give Astwood Bank a formidable score. Peter Johns, Troon's medium-pace bowler, took five for 25. Troon approached their target of 165 in gathering dusk and against a left-arm bowler of distinct pace in Joe Crumpton. Not till Terry Carter came to the wicket did the scoring rate accelerate when he promptly took 18 off Crumpton in one over, including a six into the Mound Stand. Finally, with some irony, a six from Carter into the Tavern where the Astwood Bank supporters were drowning their sorrows gave Troon the championship.

Like actors after a first night, the Troon team waited to see the press comments in the morning. I. A. R. Peebles in *The Observer* expressed some surprise, and not a little sadness, that village cricket was so professional as he looked in vain for sheep, braces and cow-pats. Dennis Compton in *The Sunday Express* hoped that

Troon won by 7 wickets

GROUND 5p

HAIG NATIONAL VILLAGE CRICKET CHAMPIONSHIP

ORGANISED BY THE CRICKETER
in conjunction with John Haig and Company Limited
and the National Cricket Association.

FINAL 1972

ASTWOOD BANK v. TROON

(40 overs-a-side—no bowler may bowl more than 9 overs)
Saturday, September, 9, 1972 (1-day Match)

ASTWOOD BANK	First Innings		Second Innings
†1 J. Yoxall	c T. Carter b Edwards..	36	
2 J. Robinson	b Thomas	30	
3 B. Spittle	b Johns	36	
4 R. Davies	st Rashleigh b Dunstan	30	
5 M. Wedgbury	l b w b Johns	0	
6 C. Robinson	b Johns	3	
7 J. Poole	l b w b Johns	0	
8 J. Crumpton	not out	16	
9 T. Bird	b Johns	1	
*10 R. Nash	not out	2	
11 F. Morrall			
	B 5, l-b 6, w , n b ,	11	B , l-b , w , n-b ,
	Total	165	Total

FALL OF THE WICKETS

1—69	2—69	3—139	4—139	5—141	6—148	7—148	8—162	9—	10—
1—	2—	3—	4—	5—	6—	7—	8—	9—	10—

ANALYSIS OF BOWLING

Name	1st Innings O.	M.	R.	W.	Wd	N-b	2nd Innings O.	M.	R.	W.	Wd.	N-b
Johns	9	1	27	5	...	...	...	...	...	...	...	...
Edwards	9	2	35	1	...	...	...	...	...	...	...	...
Thomas	9	0	35	1	...	...	...	...	...	...	...	...
Moyle	4	0	23	0	...	...	...	...	...	...	...	...
Dunstan	9	1	34	1	...	...	...	...	...	...	...	...

TROON	First Innings		Second Innings
1 J. Spry	c Poole b Morrall	2	
2 T. Edwards	b Morrall	45	
3 B. Carter	l b w b C. Robinson	19	
†4 T. Carter	not out	79	
5 J. Vincent	not out	14	
6 M. Sweeney			
7 P. Johns			
8 B. Moyle			
*9 D. Rashleigh			
10 G. Dunstan			
11 P. Thomas			
	B , l b 8, w 1, n-b 2,	11	B , l-b , w , n-b ,
	Total	170	Total

FALL OF THE WICKETS

1—14	2—50	3—117	4—	5—	6—	7—	8—	9—	10—
1—	2—	3—	4—	5—	6—	7—	8—	9—	10—

ANALYSIS OF BOWLING

Name	1st Innings O.	M.	R.	W.	Wd.	N-b	2nd Innings O.	M.	R.	W.	Wd.	N-b
Morrall	9	2	25	2	...	...	...	...	...	...	...	...
Crumpton	9	1	39	0	...	2	...	...	...	...	...	...
Yoxall	4	0	26	0	1	...	...	...	...	...	...	...
C. Robinson	6.4	1	41	1	...	...	...	...	...	...	...	...
Spittle	4	0	23	0	...	...	...	...	...	...	...	...
Bird	1	0	5	0	...	...	...	...	...	...	...	...

Umpires—L. H. Gray & H. E. Robinson Scorers—R. Pratt & T. Angove
† Captain * Wicket-keeper
Play begins at 12 noon Stumps drawn at 6.30 p.m.
Luncheon Interval 1.15 p.m.—2.15 p.m.
Tea Interval 4.15 p.m.—4.35 p.m. (may be varied according to state of game)
Troon won the toss and elected to field

The score-card at Lord's

the sponsorship of village cricket had come to stay. Michael Melford in *The Sunday Telegraph* said of Terry Carter that 'he played an innings of which none of the eminent players who have made runs on this famous ground would have been ashamed.' Perhaps the happiest man was the one who had put £50 on Troon winning when they first entered the competition.

Twelve months later Troon did it again although the victory by only 5 runs over Werrington in the first round may suggest that the gap between British village champions and the humble first-round side might not be as great as imagined. Their victims in the 1973 final were the Welshmen of Gowerton.

Their second success led to the question, put hesitantly in 1972, being asked more positively. Should a village play minor county cricketers in its side? The organisers imposed a qualified 'no' and Troon entered the 1974 competition with a ban on those who had played for a minor county or a first-class county 2nd XI within the last twelve months. As for first-class cricketers, they might never grace the village scene in the competition until they reached the age of sixty. Despite a limitation which deprived them of their current Cornwall players, Troon reached the quarter-finals in 1974. They won the whole competition again in 1976 when they defeated, with the confidence of hardened campaigners at Lord's, the Yorkshire team of Sessay, many of whom were coming to London, let alone Lord's, for the first time. Troon's opening bat in 1976 was Trevor Angove, a lad who had been scorer four years earlier. Old Steven Angove had seen it all happen.

Why Troon were so successful and what were the consequences of success, I set out to discover on an August afternoon, as I watched the club playing their old rivals, Camborne. Peter Johns, the left-arm bowler, got an early wicket with the same nagging length which had rewarded him at Lord's over the years. 'We are a very settled community,' Maurice Bolitho told me, 'men live and work locally. We have them all their cricketing lives.' Children in Troon play cricket from an early age. The game is as much part of the local scene as rugby is in the Scottish borders. It flourishes both in schools and in junior sides run by the club. 'There is an unbroken sequence up which a youngster progresses,' he added. Walter Edwards admitted the village had little else to offer and looked back to the days of the Depression. 'To play for Troon was something terrific: sought after by two hundred men on the dole whom you'd see knocking a ball up and down the village square.'

Cricket had had the same attraction for the unemployed in Nelson in Lancashire in the 1930s, when thousands paid 6d to watch an afternoon's cricket, especially if the great Learie Constantine were playing. Evidence for the link between a strong cricketing tradition and a community bitterly hit by the Depression can be found throughout the country.

Troon's success must also be attributable to a fact of Cornish cricket life: towns do not poach players from villages. Both compete on equal terms, and as the record of Troon shows, many a villager played both for the county and the village.

One of the most revealing explanations of Troon's success lay in Bolitho's comment that in thirty years as secretary he had never sent out a 'selected to play' postcard. The committee posted up the side in the village square. 'If you're playing for Troon, you turn up and find out, and see when the bus leaves.' Excuses were accepted reluctantly. Other people's weddings were frowned upon, a player's own wedding might have been better arranged, funerals were admitted but no player dared to invent one for his grandmother. 'As you clocked into the local factory, so you clocked into Troon cricket,' concluded Bolitho in reflecting on his secretaryship. 'His was a spell in office,' said Walter Edwards 'which brought Troon through thirty years with great skill. He was a pillar of strength.'

The social and economic consequences of success were significant. Troon collected prize-money of several hundred pounds in the 1970s and attracted cash through collections and raffles which added a further annual £500 on at least four occasions. 'We have no more money problems,' said one official—and how many treasurers today could echo that?

A profitable club-house already existed, a focal point for Troon's playing members and some 300 vice-presidents. Now there followed a new pavilion with well-equipped kitchen, refrigerator and showers. The ladies of the club insisted that the kitchen window should be in the front of the pavilion, and the original plans were changed.

Maurice Bolitho, Troon's secretary for many years, and the old club bag

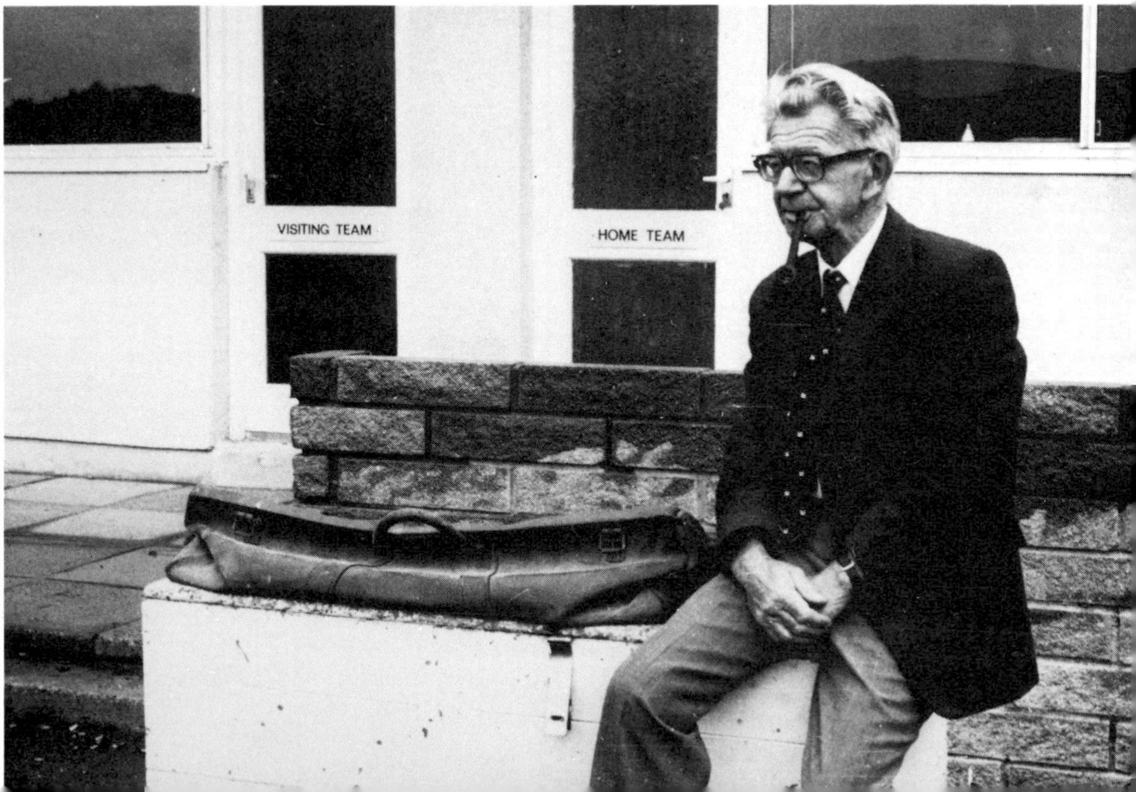

The historian of Troon cricket must beware of attributing too much to the club's success in the national village competition. The foundations of prosperity had been firmly laid already. Nevertheless, the implications of that success can be defined. Crowds turned up with their cars at 9 o'clock on a Sunday morning to get a good view of a competition match. A fringe support from the surrounding neighbourhood was attracted and retained. 'The village—and my trade—were undoubtedly changed,' remarked Walter Edwards.

Of course there were problems. In the later days of the competition, the sponsors were less generous with expenses. 'One match cost our family £100,' said Valerie Carter, Brian's wife, 'we all wanted to go, and the kids couldn't be left behind.' 'We lost a potential £750 when that train was derailed at Dawlish,' said Bolitho. 'We'd booked the train for £1,500 and sold tickets worth £2,250. We had to return the tickets and British Rail returned our fee.' For some players there was a problem of loyalty. Did David Rashleigh accept the chance of a first cap for Cornwall or play in a village tie? Everyone cheered as he boarded the coach in Troon. They also cheered when Troon brought back the silver trophy from Lord's. The Camborne town band turned out and there was a civic reception.

They cheered again as I watched David Rashleigh take a fine catch behind the stumps to dismiss Howard James, the Camborne opener, for 3. As I left the ground I took a final view. Peter Johns was bowling from the bottom end, Andrew Rashleigh was still playing with his five-year-old friends, old Steven Angove bade me come back again one day, Valerie Carter found there were too many for tea, Maurice Bolitho pointed out the old club bag of the 1930s. Beside it, a bottle of Haig lay casually in the corner. It was the spirit of victory for this twentieth-century village.

9
SUSSEX SPECTATOR

Put together a Sussex bar-billiards champion, a trustee of the village old folks' home, a craftsman who had just designed an altar cross, a retired army officer and a banker and you have one man—Frank Mitchell, for fourteen years secretary of Cuckfield Cricket Club. We met in the White Hart, where it was a Saturday custom for some of the committee to foregather. Frank had passed his secretarial responsibilities on to Roger Heavens who has got together on his committee a solicitor, a stock-broker, a bricklayer, an architect, an accountant, an insurance consultant, a carpenter, a tree surgeon, a doctor and a dentist. There can be few club decisions they cannot both make and implement themselves. The fate of nations has been decided by less formidable bodies.

From a club with such a committee you would expect paperwork of high order. Annual General Meetings are presented with balance sheets that give a break-down of club investments and stock. There was an entry in 1979 recording £35 from the sale of sausages, while their accountant had bought the club more land for £41. If you can buy real estate with bangers . . . A 2000-word report greets members as they enter the church hall in February, and a list of committee nominations for some twenty-five offices is presented to them. Those with the courage to propose alternative candidates must have done so four clear days before the meeting. All the hallmarks are there of a thoroughly efficient club, and a 'contented one', added Bob Nicholls, who had bowled from one end between the wars rather as that other Sussex cricketer, Maurice Tate, had done.

Frank Mitchell's dream had been to have a pavilion, so he negotiated the purchase of part of the grandstand at Gatwick when it was converted from a race-course to an aerodrome. Sadly, it was burnt down in 1968, and the committee had a chance to show its mettle and build a new one. Inside it, a notice told me that they hoped they had done the right thing by following Fison's advice. Time will tell. With over sixty home matches a season, sensible wicket preparation and care was vital.

The wicket, that afternoon, was almost too good as Hove Montefiore scored 250 with some ease and Cuckfield's reply was not far behind. The high scoring was in keeping with tradition. In one spectacular 'cricket week' in 1911 they topped 300 twice while their total of 334 for five declared in the 1928 week so overawed the

Cricket at Cuckfield in front of Cuckfield Park with the thirteenth-century church nearby

MCC that they fell for 117. Frank Mitchell recalled an occasion when the 2nd XI, which he captained, topped 300. 'Cuckfield went in to bat at ten-to-three and launched an amazing assault on Balcombe. Eighty-one came in half-an-hour and 150 in fifty minutes. I declared at tea with 312 on the board.' Cricket week in pre-war days was an occasion for house-parties and invitation players, a cause of 'some feeling when a 1st XI Number 1 suddenly found himself batting Number 9.' In the more democratic days of the 1970s outsiders and guests are not brought in, and Viscount Erleigh plays regularly for the 1st XI strictly on his merits.

'It's not always like that,' Roger Heavens confessed. 'We played Burgess Hill in 1960 and got them out for 8. Eight years later they came to us. After we'd lost six for 6 in six overs I went in to prop up one end. Bill Garforth departed at the other end to make it 7 for seven. In the interests of mathematical nicety, I went at eight for 8 in eight. And that was it! Burgess Hill had got their own back.'

The club owed much in its earlier days to the patronage of the Sergison family of Cuckfield Park, one of whom, Thomas, sponsored a cricket match at Cuckfield, with forty guineas as prize-money, to help him secure political support in west Sussex in the 1741 general election. Cuckfield cricketers were glad of his attentions but his parliamentary prospects had no chance against a candidate supported by the greatest political patron of the eighteenth century, the Duke of Newcastle. His political ambitions shattered, Thomas lent his social support to the club and his descendants allowed the club to play in Cuckfield Park for a peppercorn rent. The magnificent period house built by the Sergisons lies beyond the ground with its surround of pine trees and the thirteenth-century church nearby. Many a club would willingly pay more than the peppercorn rent for such a site.

I left one White Hart that evening to go to another one—the old coaching inn on the Dover-Brighton road near where the Rottingdean villagers play their cricket. Henry Blyth, president and former captain, told me of a cryptic message which left him one short before a match some years ago: 'Am in Lewes gaol. Should be available next week.' The defaulting cricketer's offence is unknown. Had it been committed in the early days of the club's history the charge of smuggling might be guessed at. For smuggling, together with fishing, was a staple occupation of Rottingdean villagers in the past, when a dangerous cliff coast-line cut them off from nearby Brighton and 'the gap' left open a path for the barrels to be rolled up from the boats.

Thomas Clare, landlord of the White Hart, must have known all about what was going on as he more openly arranged a cricket match for stakes of £5 a side. He was a good public-relations man. Cock-fighting and bull-fighting were laid on as pre-match entertainment before Squire Steyning Beard led his men out to play Henfield or Cuckfield. A Beard first led out the Rottingdean side in 1759. Three of them played against Stanmer in 1862 in a game whose score-card has survived. One of them, Ernest (at the age of seventy-six), once led the Rottingdean eleven.

Cricket Match played at Rottingdean between Rottingdean & Oving-dean Club and Stanmer Club on 18th August 1862

Rottingdean 1st First Innings

Order of going in	Name of the Batsmen	Figures as Scored	How Out	Bowler's Name	Runs
1	A. Welfare	111113	Run out (the Hon F Pelham)	T. Taylor	9
2	A Adamson		C T. Taylor	T. Taylor	0
3	Revd A Thomas	112111111	C T. Taylor	T. Taylor	11
4	S. Beard	13	Bowled	T. Taylor	4
5	G Verrall		Bowled	T. Taylor	0
6	T Beard	1211	Bowled	T. Taylor	5
7	A. Green		Bowled	T. Taylor	0
8	W Green	1112111	Bowled	T. Taylor	8
9	J Adamson		Bowled	T. Taylor	0
10	G. Beard	2	Bowled	Hon F Pelham	2
11	H Hafford		not out	—	—
	Byes	111			3
	Leg Byes				
	Wide Balls				
	No Balls				
				Total of First Innings	42

Runs at the fall of each Wicket	1 for	2 for	3 for	4 for	5 for	6 for	7 for	8 for	9 for	10 for
	2	16	23	23	29	32	33	35	42	42

The Analysis of the Bowling First Innings

Bowlers Name	No Balls	Wide Balls	The number of 'overs' and the 'runs' made from Bowlers &c.
1 Hon F. Pelham			[illegible]
2 T. Taylor			[illegible]

	Bowler's Name	Total no Balls	Total wide Balls	Total Balls	Total Runs	Total Maiden overs	Total Wickets
1	Hon F Pelham	–	–	68	19	5	1
2	T. Taylor	–	–	65	23	1	6
3							
4							

	Bowler's Names contd	Total no Balls	Total wide Balls	Total Balls	Total Runs	Total Maiden overs	Total Wickets
5							
6							
7							
8							

Notes

The score-card when Rottingdean played Ovingdean and Stanmer in 1862, in the days of four-ball overs

Trunky Thomas at Rottingdean—umpire, bathing-machine attendant, smuggler

They played their early cricket on Beacon Hill under the lee of the great windmill. That high vantage-point had announced the arrival of the Spanish Armada. When the Rottingdean cricketers played there, the beacon was part of the early-warning system against Napoleon's proposed invasion. Behind the bowler's arm at one end ships could be seen in the English Channel, and batsmen waited until they had passed by.

Napoleon never came and the cricketers went about their peaceful business consuming lunch on the Beacon Hill at 2s 6d per head with ginger beer, shandy-gaff and beer on tap all day. Danny Hyde would be umpiring at one end in his grey bowler, frock coat and light trousers, and Trunky Thomas at the other—that is, when Trunky was not attending his bathing machines or smuggling in brandy and French lace. They played on the hill for over a hundred years. It had its advantages for a batsman: someone once scored 67 off a single hit. The ball ran faster and faster down to the village, to be retrieved in the end by relays of fielders. One of them threw it with such force that the wicket-keeper missed it and it descended the hill on the other side.

Later on a roller went down the same hill. Rather than pull it up again the cricketers abandoned the beacon ground and moved, in 1914, to where they now play. Their present ground is set in a hollow and the spectators look down upon the game. 'It's a grand place for the families,' said Henry Blyth. 'They can watch in comfort and the kids can run around. A wise captain chats up the wives first, and then the players.' Blyth had raised Rottingdean sides for nearly forty years and had delighted in involving the whole community. Stanley Baldwin would watch, smoking his famous pipe. 'His future wife played. Oh yes, we had a ladies' team! We couldn't interest Rudyard Kipling. He preferred to stay at home across the road and write about 'flannelled oafs at the wicket'. Baldwin's brother-in-law, Julian, used to play wearing a cap with the tail feather of a pheasant stuck in it. He'd bring a silver bowl of rum punch to the match. Before my time, of course.

'Jack Hobbs watched in his old age and W. A. Darlington played for us, and we had a president of the MCC in his year of office turning out.'

We looked at the wicket before Rottingdean came out to field against Lindfield. It was chalky with very little subsoil. 'Some opposition captains want the heavy roller on,' said Blyth. 'Foolish, just breaks the wicket up.' Lindfield quickly lost three wickets to Michael Jackson before Norman Teague and John Rumble added 55 for the fourth wicket. Then Jackson broke through again and it was left to the Lindfield last wicket pair, David Sear and David Parry, to put together 49. In a gale-force wind off the sea Jackson had bowled for over two hours, taking eight for 68.

It took some enthusiasm that afternoon to watch cricket in the cold, but families had found themselves various sheltered spots, and people were picnicking in good

'In case anything happens to me you'll find next week's sermon in my desk. Don't forget to pay the organist . . . Miss Peewit will help you with the parish mag.' (*Cartoon by Giles, London Express Service*)

British style. There were anoraks and scarves and thick tartan rugs. Flasks of tea and coffee appeared and children were summoned from the hinterland to dispose of Marmite sandwiches. Less brave spirits ate in the comfort of their cars. One stout-hearted fellow announced he would walk down the village street for a breath of sea-air. I asked if there was a member of the Beard family playing. 'No,' they told me, 'no Beard today, nor a Dudeney [*Dieu donné*—God given], nor a Sladescane.' I found out that the modern Rottingdean cricketer isn't one of the old families whose names go back to the Domesday Book. They are commuters to London—accountants, publishers, stock-brokers, solicitors. But the secretary, Humphrey Elcock, was determined to keep it a village club. 'We want it that way,' he added. Elcock is a surgeon, a busy man with a gift for delegating. 'I was against his being secretary,' said his wife Aileen (Brighton Ladies' tennis champion), not very convincingly. She had rejoiced in the success of the club's match against the Variety Club All-Stars XI. 'We raised a lot for charity as well as for the club.'

'We need a lot of money. We rent the ground,' said the secretary. 'It costs £300 to have the out-field cut and the rates on the pavilion are another £200.' Henry Blyth remembered when a piebald pony was used to cut the field, pulling the mowers of a local farmer. A pony passed us by, bearing a young lady as the Rottingdean side went out to chase the Lindfield total of 158. Three wickets fell quickly before John Lawrence pulled the innings together. Despite his 25, the game seemed to be going Lindfield's way and I made mine to Henfield.

'Henfield? Our old rivals! Their butcher once dropped a vital catch against us and no one in Henfield bought his meat for a week.' Blyth's memories went back nearly fifty years—a busy cricket career interspersed with writing film-scripts for J. Arthur Rank.

To see cricket at Henfield is to tread on the commons land on which they have played for over 250 years. Farmer Thomas Marchant wrote in his diary in 1721, 'Will and Terry went to a cricket match at Henfield.'

A later diarist, John Baker, had a day out in July 1773, arriving in the rain when Horsham had set Henfield 104 to win:

> Kidd immediately catched out by Bigg, and then Beauchamp one more and next ball run out by falling down. The only two poor ones left and then Poulton catched out one by a fine catch when they lost by 25 notches.

The club on the gorse-clad common regards 1771 as the date of its first formal organisation. Sixty-six years later, in 1837, the committee drew up a revised list of rules which included the remarkably high subscription of 5s a year—especially when set against the 1979 subscription of £1.

But the earlier committee members had other ways of raising revenue: 'In practice, every member not fetching 5 runs in each innings shall be forfeit a penny,' and 'any member degrading himself and party by getting to liquor before the match is played out, he is under the forfeit of 2s 6d' (half the year's subscription!).

The reconstituted club quickly became the strongest in the county so that the Sussex side would sometimes take the field with a large number of Henfield men. When the village played Hampshire in 1848 (and had much the best of the draw) ten of the Henfield XI were county players. One of the stars of those years was Henry Charlwood who scored the club's first century and whose third-wicket partnership with Richard Fillery of 211 against Brighton in 1865 is still the club's third-wicket record.

Perhaps the close association with the county, and the production of thirty-two county players in Victorian times, became an embarrassment. A resolution of the committee in 1880 declared that: 'the club would be run on the lines of modern village cricket; local players should have first call on a place in the team and conditions would be made as easy as possible for them to get a game.'

As a 'modern village cricket club' Henfield has continued to flourish with a record of success which must be the envy of most other sides. It is a club proud of its past, as a wall of mounted and framed pictures in the pavilion bears testimony, but it lives in the present. 'The youngsters are as interested now as when we were young,' commented one club official, 'and we do all we can to encourage them.'

'Excuse me while I have a word with this Mod about transistor radios' (*Cartoon by Giles, London Express Service*)

'I trod historic ground'—John Reid's painting of village cricket in Ashington in Sussex in 1878 (*The Tate Gallery, London*)

Henfield draws the crowd as much from its own long and rambling village as from those further afield who come to the commons with their peaceful surroundings of silver birch, oak and hawthorn. 'Half of them come to watch the cricket, the other half to kick a football around and have a drink in the bar afterwards.' It was a realistic comment from a player who explained why the subscription remained so low. 'We take a collection from them.' Len McKinnon ran the bar, served on the committee and believed the MCC had never beaten Henfield. It would take a lot of proving one way or the other.

I watched Henfield play Ifield. Both clubs had one thing in common. Farmer Marchant had recorded in his diary their early spectators. Will had gone with Jack (instead of Terry) 'to Ifield Green to see a cricket match.' In 1784 the annual Henfield-Ifield encounter at Henfield had been enlivened by a running match between 'Mr Hewat of Henfield and Mr Flint of Ifield for 60 guineas.' 'We sorted them out fifty years ago, in 1928,' an Ifield player told me gleefully. 'We got 173 for nought and put them out for 25.' Men had been coming from Ifield down Sussex lanes to play men at Henfield for 200 years. I trod historic ground.

But then, most of Sussex village cricket is historic. Not far from Henfield and Ifield lies Slindon where the Duke of Richmond, grandson of Charles II and Louise de Querouaille, ran the side which, at the height of its fame, beat Surrey! The Duke, in great delight, wrote to a fellow duke: 'poore little Slyndon against almost your whole county!'

Slindon's matches, of course, attracted the punters, and a typical hand-bill showed the club's fame:

> On Monday September 6 1742, will be played at Artillery Ground, the greatest match at cricket that has been played for many years between the famous parish of Slyndon in Sussex and eleven picked gentlemen of London. And 'tis expected there will be the greatest crowd by reasons of the very large sums of money which is laid.

Later, Richard Nyren took over the captaincy, but the fortunes of Slindon declined when he departed across the county border to Hambledon in Hampshire to become the 'general' of that club. Meanwhile, the Duke of Richmond had been posted to military duties, defending the Hanoverian government against the Jacobites. Had Nyren stayed in Sussex and Richmond not gone north the story of Slindon might have been that of Hambledon.

My final pilgrimage was to Storrington, yet another eighteenth-century Sussex club by the Downs. No longer was it the remote village, set in a quiet lane with smoke curling from quaint cottages, immortalised by Hugh de Sélincourt in his books as Tillingfold. Now a modern breeze-block pavilion stands firmly guarding the frontier between cricket and football fields. A housing estate flanks one side and traffic on the busy road to Pulborough passes ceaselessly by on the other. Here de Sélincourt had loved his cricket between the wars. They had played with stumps

'Storrington v Tillingfold': the Storrington side in 1937; Cecil Waller is on the left with right hand folded across his chest, Hugh de Sélincourt is inset. Many of the side were the originals of de Sélincourt's Tillingfold characters

painted pure white. There was no marked boundary and batsmen frequently ran fives to the northern end.

One August, de Sélincourt and Cecil Waller managed to play on twenty-eight days. Tea was brewed on a Primus stove, and water fetched from across the road. After seeing them on different occasions in the 'colours' of Storrington, the Kenya Kongonis and Littlehampton, the elder George Cox, the Sussex cricketer, asked, 'Who the devil do you chaps play for?' 'Any one who is kind enough to ask us, and sometimes we just turn up if we think that someone may be short of a couple.' Then came the war. De Sélincourt hated war—he abhorred (he said) blackshirts and brownshirts, and lived for white shirts.

Waller's war was spent playing for the Sussex Home Guard eleven, keeping the cricket ground in trim, instructing air cadets, offering cricket to servicemen and (in his spare time) being headmaster of a school of 600. Waller usually got five wickets a match—the ones that Joe Page didn't get at the other end, the 'original' of de Sélincourt's Sid Smith.

I had reached Storrington too late to see any cricket. Perhaps it was best that way. The summer evening shadows fell on the village ground, the traffic died away, the harsh contours of functional architecture became blurred. Peace descended. Maybe out in the middle, the shades were playing the most improbable match of all—Storrington v. Tillingfold.

10
VILLAGE CRICKET IN FICTION

Cricket has made a noble contribution to English literature. No game can match its fine array of poets and prose-writers. They have talked of Grace, Fry and Ranji, of Rhodes and Hirst, of Roses matches and festivals at Canterbury, of Bradman's centuries at Worcester and September cup-match crowds at Lord's. No man in a lifetime could read all the literature of the game were he to dispatch his television to a distant corner on winter evenings (he would want it back in May) and bid his family farewell as he entrenched himself in his library. If he is to sustain his role as a balanced and well-disposed individual whose life has many facets, let him be selective. He might, for example, contemplate the literature of village cricket.

Not long after the Hambledon cricketers were playing on Broad-Halfpenny Down, and not far away, Mary Russell Mitford was living on the Hampshire-Berkshire border. She was a playwright and an essayist, and her work included *Our Village*, which appeared in five volumes from 1824 onwards.

Mary Mitford's delight in watching village cricket shows itself in her chapter on the match against Bramley. The village team desperately needs James Brown, a journeyman-blacksmith who had left home because Mary Allen had rejected him. Her letter brings him back:

> Mistur Browne this is to Inform yew that oure parish plays bramley men next monday is a week, i think we shall lose without yew, from your humbell servant to command. MARY
> MARY ALLEN

Mary Allen has relented and James Brown returns to play alongside Ben Appleton, whose 'abilities at cricket were not completely ascertained but so full of fun and waggery; no doing without Ben'; alongside William Grey, 'a farmer's son by station and an excellent cricketer'; alongside Samuel Long 'who owns one cow, two donkeys, six pigs, ducks beyond count and so steady a player! So safe!' The village wins—despite the rain—and everyone departs, 'the players to their supper and we to our homes: all wet through, all good humoured and all happy—except the losers. Who would think that a little bit of leather and two pieces of wood had such a delightful and delighting power?'

It was a power which appealed to Mr Pickwick and the fellow members of the

'Out! So don't fatigue yourself, I beg, sir.' Cricket—Pickwickian style (*MCC*)

Pickwick Club who watched Dingley Dell play All-Muggleton. As Gentlemen from London, they were treated as honoured guests and escorted to the tent—'they notch in here, it's the best place in the whole field.' There they met Alfred Jingle whose staccato conversation outlined the day's pleasures: 'Capital fun—lots of beer—hogsheads; rounds of beef—bullocks, mustard—cartloads; glorious day—down with you—make yourself at home—glad to see you—very.'

Charles Dicken's Pickwickians settled down to watch All-Muggleton bat and his readers enjoy the opening two runs of the innings:

> All-Muggleton had the first innings; and the interest became intense when Mr Dumkins and Mr Podder, two of the most renowned members of that most distinguished club,

walked bat in hand to their respective wickets. 'Play!' suddenly cried the bowler. The ball flew from his hand straight and swift towards the centre stump of the wicket. The wary Dumkins was on the alert; it fell upon the tip of his bat, and bounded far away over the heads of the scouts, who had just stooped low enough to let it fly over them.

'Run—Run—another—. Now, then throw her up—up with her—stop there—another—no—yes—no—throw her up, throw her up!' Such were the shouts which followed the stroke; and at the conclusion of which All-Muggleton had scored two. Nor was Podder behind-hand in earning laurels wherewith to garnish himself and Muggleton. He blocked the doubtful balls, missed the bad ones, took the good ones, and sent them flying to all parts of the field. The scouts were hot and tired; the bowlers were changed and bowled till their arms ached; but Dumkins and Podder remained unconquered.

All-Muggleton's eventual 54 was too much for Dingley Dell though the margin of defeat was not revealed. Mr Jingle's, 'Ah, Ah—stupid—Now, butter-fingers—Muff—Humbug,' during the course of the match had made him something of an authority on the game and earned him an invitation to join the party for dinner at the Blue Lion, especially when he admitted to having played cricket in the West Indies and scored 570 in a single-wicket contest.

Dickens' other references to the village game are incidental. Tom Pinch, in *Martin Chuzzlewit*, makes a coachride up to London one summer's evening, passing hedges, gates and trees, people going home from work, churches in quiet nooks and village greens 'where cricket players linger yet'. In *Sunday Under Three Heads* 'the boys and young men are playing while girls, ladies and old people are watching the progress of the game.' An old clergyman approaches. Will he stop the game—for it is a Sunday and not all clerics were sympathetic? And then we are told that the 'clergyman himself had established the whole thing—that it was his field they played in, and that it was he who had purchased stumps, bats, ball and all.'

Dickens took the simplistic view of village cricket and delighted to play and to be a scorer himself. Another Victorian novelist, George Meredith, took a more lofty tone and drew upon village cricket to convey several viewpoints to his readers. He saw the England of his day as still rigidly feudal in social attitudes and he felt cricket could help to break this down. He also regarded the men as condescending to their womenfolk. And he believed in national pride and personal endeavour. In *Evan Harrington*

the sons of first-rate families are in the two elevens mingled with the yeomen, and whoever can do best the business. Fallowfield and Beckley, without regard to rank, have drawn upon their muscle and science. One of the bold men of Beckley at the wickets is Nick Frim, son of the gamekeeper at Bickley Court: the other is young Tom Copping, son of Squire Copping, of Dox Hall in the parish of Beckley. Nick and Tom were stretching from post to post, might and main. It is good to win glory for your country; it is also good to win glory for your village.

But the squire of Fallowfield was ready to snub the lady who applauded Beckley's batting.

> 'What a beautiful hit!' exclaimed one of the ladies languidly watching the ascent of the ball.
>
> 'Beautiful, d'ye call it,' muttered the Squire.
>
> The ball, indeed, was dropping straight into the hand of the long-hit-off. Instantly a thunder rolled. But it was Beckley that took the joyful treble—Fallowfield the deeply-cursing bass. The long-hit-off, he who never was known to miss a catch—butter-fingered beast!—he has let the ball slip through his finger.

And so the lady has the last laugh.

In *Diana of the Crossways*, Diana Merion, watching a village match, envies the masculinity and prowess of Tom Redworth (her eventual husband). 'I think the chief advantage men have over us is in their amusements.' When her friend Emma Dunstane comments that Tom is the sort of father who would play cricket with his sons, Diana tartly adds 'and lock up his daughters in the nursery'. But men did not play cricket unfettered. Emma Dunstane's husband, Sir Lukin, indicates that marriage has ended his cricket. 'My stumps are down: I'm married.'

Village cricket for Meredith was a chance to indulge in something essentially English and to have a few sly digs at foreigners. In *Evan Harrington* success in cricket does not turn the heads of the English, 'as it would of frivolous foreigners'. In *The Adventures of Harry Richmond* the stage-coach driver tells his passenger that foreigners 'had a bit of an idea that cricket was the best game in the world, though it was a nice joke to see a foreigner playing at it.' The driver—a man condemned to inactivity in the perpetual act of motion—gives his idea of happiness:

> Cricket in cricket season! It comprises—count: lots o' running; and that's good; just enough o' taking it easy; that's good: a appetite for your dinner, and your ale or your port, as may be the case; good, number three. Add on a tired pipe after dark, and a sound sleep to follow, and you say good morning to the doctor and the parson: for you're in health body and soul, and ne'er a parson'll make a better Christian of ye, that I'll swear.

Sir George Lowton, the MP in *Evan Harrington*, thinks that village cricket contributes to 'local rivalries, local triumphs—the strength of the kingdom,' while Sir Lukin Dunstane conducts a running commentary on the Copsley estate team's batting interspersed with his views on national pride.

National pride, or the glory of the village: Meredith extols both. His love of the game is evident. He was an outdoor man himself, a walker, climber, sailor and boxer. But, like many of his fellow Victorians, he was a moralist as well. At bottom, there is a moral fervour in much of what he writes. As a mountaineer he knew the need for training and the dire consequences of error. Many of his subjects are in moral training so that they shall live better lives, or solve particular problems or simply hold their end up; 'the two last men of an eleven are twins; they hold one life between them, so that he who dies extinguishes the other.' Cricket asks that much of the tail-ender!

A rather different hint at the virtues or vices of playing village cricket lies in a strange little book written by Phoebe Allen in 1884 and called *The Cricket Club or Warned in Time. A story for mothers' meetings.*

Jack and Jenny Down live in the village of Mapledene where Jack is a good-natured, long-suffering carpenter whose only vice is playing cricket. Jenny, once a pretty young girl who had admired his talents on the field, is a tired young mother with small children about her and a nagging tongue. One day Jack collapses on the field of play. Jenny's reaction is to hope he will have the sense to give up the game. He doesn't, and soon afterwards, collapses again. This time it proves fatal. Jenny is distraught with grief and wishes she had been a better wife. As the reader comes to share her misery, so he shares her joy. Jack's second collapse had happened in her dreams! As in any good fairy-story they now live happily ever after: 'No more grumbling or fretting or complaining; no more sulking if he went out to his cricket practice; no more reproaches if he took a shilling for his club expenses.' Truly a moral tale with just a hint of chauvinism about it.

Much of English village cricket reveals the benevolence of the parson. He appears as both patron and player. He usually smiles kindly on the scene and, as Mr Punch once observed, is ready to appoint as his curate one who can bowl—in the days, of course, when villages had curates.

But H. G. Wells, in *Certain Personal Matters*, produced the person whom the ancient village cricketer (now just an umpire) could not get on with:

> A well meaning, earnest and exceedingly nervous young man; the worst of all possible rural vicars, no classical scholar, no lover of nature. He was meant to labour among urban myriads, to deal with social evils, Home Rule, the Woman Question and the Reunification of Christendom. Him my cricketer regards with malignant respect by a punctilious touching of his hat brim, directed to the sacred office; all the rest is malignity.

They came in contact on the field. For the vicar is 'conscious of his duty to encourage cricket by participation'. Then the vicar committed his worst crime, 'to discuss the ancient's chickens with him when that worthy was umpiring—What would the vicar think if the cricketer discussed the vicarage pony during a pause in the sermon?'

Most village clubs have their ancient cricketer. He snarls from the boundary (better there than as an umpire—for his umpiring will be either partial when it should be impartial, or indifferent in skill when it should be indifferent in loyalties). He turns up for tea, noisily consuming through ill-fitting teeth. He complains to the secretary that the side is one short (as if that poor worthy hasn't tried hard to get that last man). Worst of all (as Wells puts it) he 'abounds in reminiscence of the glorious days that have gone for ever . . .' Wells' ancient cricketer recollected cricketers in beaver hats and himself running 'a matter of four miles after a day's work in the garden where he was employed, to attend an hour's practice before twilight made the ball invisible.' We need not deplore his athleticism so long as he allows us to turn up in our cars.

But, of course, Wells' ancient cricketer has to reminisce 'of gallant stands and unexpected turns of fortune, of memorable hits, albeit sometimes incredibly to his glory.' We must not carp; he has little else left except the memory 'of eleven men in a drag, and tuneful homecomings by the light of the moon.' His village was a home and nursery of stalwart cricketers.

Those who wrote upon cricket, and those who played it in the villages came together towards the end of the nineteenth century in a team founded and captained by J. M. Barrie, the author of *Peter Pan.* The side called itself the 'Allahakbarries', the first part of the word bearing some relation to an African word for 'Heaven help us!' and the second half representing the followers of Barrie, at least as cricketers.

One view of normalcy:
Incoming batsman (to deep field): 'Er—am I going right for the wicket, please?' (*Punch*)

Barrie's team included J. C. Snaith, whose *Willow the King* just touches the fringes of village cricket, William Meredith, son of George, Conan Doyle, creator of Sherlock Holmes, E. V. Lucas, editor of *Punch*, and A. E. W. Mason. Their first match was against the Surrey village of Shere who dismissed them for 11. Perhaps Shere felt the newly-born fledgling might not survive such a tragedy. At any rate, their ground was offered to the Allahakbarries and gratefully accepted.

Barrie soon realised that the more distinguished a man was as an author, the less well did he perform on the field. So that Mason, a fast bowler, was as likely 'to send the bails flying as to hit square leg in the stomach'. Only when Barrie

A second view of normalcy: 'And the best of it is I'm not out for eight months' (*MCC*)

'surreptitiously introduced', as he tells us in *The Greenwood Hat*, outsiders (men who didn't write) did the Allahakbarries 'occasionally astound the tented field'.

Barrie never wrote anything specifically on village cricket but a few lines must be spared to describe his single-wicket match with his young friend David, near the Round Pond in Kensington Gardens.

> We did not exactly pitch stumps for they were forbidden in the gardens but we selected a ragged yew. David's bowling was underarm and not exactly elegant, but sometimes he tried a round-arm which doubled up square-leg—only there was no one fielding at square-leg, or anywhere else.

David and Barrie completed a first innings each. J. M. Barrie fell for 5 but David, with 'two pretty drives for 3 both behind the wicket' reached 9. J. M. Barrie's second innings brought him 23 and left David 19 to get. 'As I gave him the bat, he looked brave, but something wet fell on my hand and then a sudden fear seized me lest David should not win.' David survived a yorker hitting the yew ('Not out,' cried J. M. Barrie), and a dropped catch off the bowler. He went on to win 'with two lovely fours, pelting home to his mother with the glorious news'.

Many small boys, bored with the stern encounter being waged on the village green (*their* green on other days of the week), have fought similar tussles on the sidelines.

Barrie's cricketers take us into the twentieth century and to a group of writers who belong to the years between the two world wars. After the First World War, the desperate pursuit of 'normalcy'—the return to a world where people live decent, ordinary but fulfilled lives—brought great enthusiasm for sport and the use of leisure. Cricket came back to the villages although it met some challenge from the growth of amateur football leagues and from the new sports of motoring, cycling or walking in the countryside.

Three writers who lived through the experience of the First World War (two of them had fought in it) turned to the theme of village cricket. Their scene is set in the 1920s and 1930s. They take a common delight in the pleasure of simple things. Nature smiles kindly on their cricketers. Whatever economic hardships life may still offer, these stand no comparison with the horrors of war. Friendship and humanity, loyalty and sportsmanship are cardinal virtues. We may smile—at a distance of fifty or sixty years—at some of the characterisation of individuals. We may condemn the reluctance to accept change. But we must accept that Hugh de Sélincourt, A. G. Macdonnell and R. C. Sherriff were portraying a rural world whose values were deeply cherished.

Hugh de Sélincourt set his various cricket books in the village of Storrington which he called Tillingfold, lying in a fold under the Sussex Downs whose sweet air put gossip to shame and whose friendly peacefulness made discontent remote.

Dear little cottages looked out over the mill pond. We are lulled into a gentle acceptance of Tillingfold—the village we would like to live in. De Sélincourt thought so too: 'No wonder bungalows are springing up on all sides.' Our bungalow would, no doubt, have all mod cons. The mill-pond cottages shared 'one latrine conspicuously outside—the bucket emptied once a week.'

Edgar Trine's home in the village was rather better appointed. At eight o'clock Kate the housemaid awoke him on the morning of the match against Raveley.

> 'It's eight o'clock, sir,' said the neat housemaid as she set the morning tea-tray on the bed-table, by the side of Edgar Trine.
>
> 'Oh, thanks, Kate, thanks,' said Trine, turning sleepily over.
>
> Kate went noiselessly on the thick carpet, pulling back one heavy curtain after another.
>
> 'I say, pour me out a cup of tea, Kate,' came a nice voice from the bed.
>
> 'Sugar and milk. Yes, I do hate pouring out tea. I'd almost rather not drink it than pour it out for myself.'
>
> 'You might ask James to bring the two-seater round about quarter-past-two, will you? And I say, do look and see if I've a decent pair of white trousers. Perhaps you wouldn't mind fetching them out of the drawer and letting me have a look.'
>
> Kate brought five pairs and laid them on the bed.

Two hours earlier Kate's brother-in-law had himself woken up, picked a Woodbine out of its paper on the mantelpiece, got dressed and put on his working boots in the scullery. Small children had swarmed around, demanded pennies, unwittingly dragged his cricket flannels across the floor and hampered the harassed Mrs Smith as she prepared Sid's bread and dripping.

Tillingfold as imagined in the first edition of de Sélincourt's *The Game of the Season*

'Where in hell are them trousers?' he cried.

'How should I know where you put 'em? They were mended last night, that's all I know.'

'Blast it!' he cried. 'What's this? Look here.'

And rising slowly, he lifted the forlorn, soiled trousers. Dismay extinguished the anger on his face. It was only on the cricket field that Sid Smith, a bowler famed for many miles around, was able to feel a man's self-respect.

'I say, Liz, wash 'em through for me, old gal.'

And Sid was off on his three-mile walk to his work as a bricklayer's caddy.

De Sélincourt's gifts lay in characterisation: the good-natured if prosperous Trine, Sid Smith who fulfilled himself only when bowling, sulky Bill Wishart wanting more than anything else in the world to play but resentful at being asked at the last moment, the sensitive, artistic skipper, Paul Gauvinier ('Lord! who'd run a side!'), old John McLeod, round and chubby and immensely proud of his new cap and dotingly cared for by his Maria.

Part of it is a world of make-believe, as when the village beat the Australians. The Champions of 1921—who vanquished England three-none in the 'Test' series—fell to Tillingfold for a paltry 39, and then created a very favourable impression as they walked with their hands on the roller while Tillingfold did the rolling. It is also a realistic world: 'Young fellers don't seem so keen nowadays. These here pickchers and them motor-cycles,' say the old cricketers. Most of all it sets out to be a better world, deserved by those who had been through Armageddon and those whose youth spared them its horrors.

A. G. Macdonnell's *England, Their England* tells the story of the Scots gunner subaltern, Donald Cameron, who had served on the Western Front and eventually set out to collect material for a book on the English, at the suggestion of a Welsh subaltern who was a publisher in private life. One of his first experiences was to play cricket for the literary team being raised by William Hodge. Donald found himself one Saturday morning boarding a charabanc at the Embankment.

The date was somewhere in the 1920s and the bus was bound for Fordenden in Sussex. What follows is a piece of romantic escapist literature. As the team leaves the charabanc Donald espies rural England: 'The real England, unspoilt by factories and financiers and tourists and hustle.' The sun, of course, shines. 'It was a hot summer's afternoon. There was no wind, and the smoke from the red-roofed cottages curled slowly up into the golden haze. Bees lazily drifted.' And the setting is all Donald could have wished for, 'for there stood the Vicar, beaming absent-mindedly at everyone. There was the forge, with the blacksmith, his hammer discarded, tightening his snake-buckled belt for the fray and loosening his braces to enable his terrific bowling-arm to swing freely in its socket.' The scenario was completed by a row of elderly men outside the Three Horseshoes, 'facing a row of pint tankards, and wearing either long beards or clean-shaven chins and long whiskers.' So the villagers waited for the great match to begin: 'a match against gentlemen from London is an event . . . Doves cooed. The haze flickered. The world stood still.'

There, as the world stood still, was the contrast to the 'maelstrom of noise and mud and death' with which Macdonnell's novel had begun. Cricket in an English village was the return to normalcy.

On the whole, Macdonnell reserves his humour for the 'gentlemen from London' rather than the village side. Robert Southcott, a famous novelist, bidden to play carefully by his skipper, dispatches the ball all over the ground. For Donald Cameron read Macdonnell himself, and for Robert Southcott read Alec Waugh, for whom the village cricket of *England, their England* 'was like that quite often'.

The third writer was the playwright R. C. Sherriff. Sherriff's *Journey's End*, performed in 1929, was the first play on the London stage to face the public with the horrors of the war upon which they had turned their backs.

A year later, Sherriff's play *Badger's Green* was produced. Badger's Green is a small Hampshire village where Sherriff dutifully presents us with appropriate characterisation—gentry, retired soldiery and villagers. Their peaceful existence and the undisturbed tenor of their ways is challenged by the arrival of Mr Butler, a speculative builder, who has issued a prospectus for the 'Badger's Green development Syndicate' which proposes 'perfectly constructed bungalows', a golf course, a cinema, a dance hall, a sanitary laundry, a Japanese tea garden and a park for charabancs.

Butler's bombshell fell two days before Badger's Green played Ragholt. Sherriff offers us what we have come to expect, as of right. It is the 'local derby' fought out on a baking day in a setting (Mr Butler is told) one would never forget: 'smooth green, the great elms around it, the old houses peering out of the shade, the lovely quiet Downs beyond, old Hobson's mare watching over a gate, people lying under the trees, the glorious firm "chock" of the ball against the bat.' There is the exciting finish in which the home team needs 2 to win with the last man in. What writer of cricket fiction ever confers a ten-wickets' defeat on the team of his fancy or takes his readers through to an unsatisfying draw in a day punctuated by showers and presided over by leaden clouds?

Sherriff completes the picture of good will. The winning hit was scored by the speculative Butler, pressed into service at the last moment. Everyone goes to the Blue Boar to celebrate. The first round is on Butler, a newly-elected vice-president who announces that he will 'build somewhere else'. Badger's Green remains undisturbed. We need not concern ourselves with the fate of the village somewhere else; it probably didn't have a cricket club anyway.

One further writer of this period deserves to be noticed. John Moore, writing after the Second World War, looked back to the thirties in his *Brensham Village*, set in Gloucestershire.

The author joined the village cricket club because his first innings was appreciated—a six first ball and out the second.

'That's the sort of innings we like to see at Brensham,' they said. 'Afterwards we all went to the "Adam and Eve" and played darts.' He liked the little ground with the sight of apple-blossom, the smell of bat-oil and the sound of plates being washed up by Mini and Meg, 'two merry little blondes'.

Moore's fellow players are rather less conventional village characters. Sammy Hunt, the captain, was a sailor who had retired to Brensham because it was 'on a puddling little river'. He would direct his bowlers as if he were still afloat: 'pitch the beggar on the starboard side'. Alfie Perks was secretary, a fruit grower who worried neither about his harvest nor his teams. He knew who would turn out, who would 'dig in their gardens, fiddle with their motor-bikes or take their wenches to the pictures.' Jeremy Briggs the blacksmith was a socialist who was *not* a mighty smiter. Then there was the Potterer. On the field he pottered about dropping catches. Off it he pottered about gardening, catching butterflies and building rock-gardens. One day the Potterer got knighted for past services to hydraulic engineering in the Far East. Brensham's scorer was a postman-cum-poacher.

There is, as we must expect, a village match. Brensham beat Woody Burton by 1 run off the last ball. Briggs the blacksmith has to catch a skier, so high that he has time to put matches and pipe in his pocket before securing it. War comes, and Sammy Hunt goes back to sea and aircraft factories come to Brensham. Cricket is laid aside but it will one day return—part of the 'imponderable, indestructible things of life'. Moore is one of the romantics.

Village cricket in the setting of the last two generations finds writers in E. N. Simons and John Parker. Cricket in a Derbyshire village after the Second World War is the subject of E. N. Simons' *Friendly Eleven*. He has the courage to stage a match in which only one ball is bowled before the rain comes down. He has opinions on why the ladies watch the village play. Wives go to ensure their husbands don't spend too long in the pub or pay too much attention to pretty visiting ladies. They go to defend their men against 'rude remarks from hostile spectators, to knit, to gossip, and to knit.' Sweethearts are there to be with their boys, to watch out for 'piratical hussies from other villages' and to see if 'the Romeo of their secret unfulfilled dreams is in the opposition'. Unattached girls are there 'to become attached as quickly as possible'. The ladies beat the men in the annual match and so preserve 'peace in the home and village, and in the long run that may be the greater victory'.

Of all the writers on village cricket in the twentieth century, Simons is the realist. His players have bad spells and his description of the elderly cricketer's last innings is sombre. The old player makes 'a 10 whose shakiness the numerals in the score-book will never reveal.' He walks out of the game as a lad cries, 'That wer' thi last innin's, warn'it, Mester.'

John Parker took up the mantle of Tillingfold in 1977, in *The Village Cricket Match*, forty years on from de Selincourt's day. Edgar Trine is now Colonel Sir Edgar, a man with a good war record, chairman of numerous committees and of Tillingfold Cricket Club. Gauvinier, the artistic and sensitive captain of the thirties, fell at Dunkirk. His son, Peter, in advertising, is now the skipper. No longer is there the rotund figure of old John McLeod with his wife, Maria, fussing over him. The present secretary is James Mitterman, a chartered accountant who catches the 7.40 to Victoria each day and wonders if he can go on living in Tillingfold if *The Times* continues to be late.

So life is different. It is expensive—bats cost £20. It is complicated—a letter with VAT demands threatens to spoil Bill Budgeon's day against Raveley. It is permissive—young Edward Trine sleeps with the au pair. It is multi-racial—two of the Raveley side are Pakistanis and one a Jamaican.

Yes! Tillingfold still play Raveley. The 1977 encounter is the 113th between them, 49 victories apiece. Raveley, indeed, has scant claims to being a village any more. From being a place 'with a couple of pubs, a green, a cricket pitch, a church and a history,' it has become 'a series of brick and breeze-block houses, concrete walkways and a modern shopping centre.'

Tillingfold has fared less badly at the hands of planners and developers and (Gauvinier admits) is not picturesque enough to attract the tourists.

The weather is kind for the match. Tillingfold win by a wicket with two balls left. Gauvinier makes a 50 with the same tension and outburst of nervous energy with which his father had batted. The Dog and Duck is still there and not very much changed. Players drink their beer there after the game. Mary Mitford, Mr Pickwick, Wells' ancient cricketer and the rest of them would not be out of place.

11
THE SECRETARY'S YEAR

The church bells of Cricket St Bede rang in the New Year and the villagers drank each other's health in the Bat and Ball.

'Funny sort of year, last year,' said George. 'Rained all May, a grand strawberry crop in June, and fine weather for the harvest. Wonder what this year will bring us! What with the EEC and the Green Pound, I don't know where farmers will be.'

'Cheer up, George, and drink up,' replied Arthur, treasurer of the cricket club and an accountant at a nearby sausage firm. 'No need to worry yet: the New Year's only just begun. Time for you farmers to start worrying if there's snow at lambing time.'

'Worse if the snow comes in May,' interrupted Brian, the club's secretary, 'just as we're trying to get the season off to a good start. Nothing worse than snow to put off the faint-hearted.'

'Got any new players then, to take their place?' asked Arthur.

'Who's taking whose place?' Peter, a lorry-driver and the oldest in the group, was on the offensive. Last summer he had announced that he wouldn't be pushed into retiring, but he still viewed all newcomers with suspicion.

'Not to worry, Peter. We'll fit you in all right. You're still one of the regulars. It's the chaps who reckon the season starts when the sun comes out and it's warm on their backs who get on *my* back,' replied Brian. 'They want a game in June against Pellington, but won't turn out against Fauxton in May.'

'Steady on, old man,' broke in John, a bank clerk, 'getting a bit personal, aren't we? Just because I refused to play on that cow-patch Fauxton call a track. Who helped you out when you needed another player to drive in the rain to Lessingham? Eighty-five miles, two quid for match-fee and lunch, watched the rest of you bat, more rain at tea, and that was that. Never even put my boots on.'

'You're all right, John,' said Brian, 'a secretary can always do with a few last-minute chaps like you, who don't get upset at a phone call . . .'

'And whose wives don't either,' interrupted Eileen, a long-suffering cricket widow who saw her husband at weekends only if she did the teas.

The inhabitants of Cricket St Bede gradually dispersed and braced themselves to face the New Year.

Brian was a schoolmaster, an occupation which allowed him one or two days'

New Year's Day (*Cartoon by Michael Bird*)

grace before he returned to work and the spring term. He had always valued the extra leisure that teachers got. He wouldn't let you get away with the argument that the job ended at 4 p.m., and would produce a pile of books awaiting correction to show his critics. But he accepted that teachers could find a little time which others couldn't, and he used his towards helping the community. That was why he was secretary of the village cricket club.

Next morning he wandered up to the ground—bleak, wet and recently denuded of its ring of elm trees. 'Not a pretty sight,' he reflected. 'Stumps of elms sticking out of the ground, great scars across the out-field from the lorries taking the wood away.'

'Talking to yourself, then?' said a voice over his shoulder, 'first sign of madness, they say.'

'Hullo, Arthur, didn't see you arrive. Usually wander up here on New Year's Day, just to see what had to be done.'

'New Year's Day? You're up here every day on some pretext or other. Well, there's not much you can do about those elms. Old Vince remembers them being planted. Vince was just a lad then but he remembers the gaps there were in the hedges. I think he said it was the parson who got the new ones planted. Hundred-and-fifty-year life those elms would have had if this Dutch disease hadn't killed 'em. Why "Dutch" anyway?'

'The disease started there—laid Holland almost bare about fifty years ago, that's why.'

'Serves 'em right for not playing cricket.'

'Ah, there you're wrong, Arthur. The Dutch *do* play cricket. They and the Danes are the only two countries in Europe that do.'

'Hope for the EEC yet,' contributed George, who had joined them.

'Talking about the Dutch,' said Brian, 'I was thinking about a tour to Holland next year. Take a bit of planning, but we could get a package trip—charter flight to the Hague, two or three games, they're a keen lot, play on matting. Do you know in 1944, five years after the German occupation, they were still able to kit themselves out in full whites? I saw a picture once, some Dutch schoolboys' eleven.'

George and Arthur were impressed. If Brian had a Dutch tour in mind, then a Dutch tour there would be. Arthur, the treasurer, wondered how much it would cost.

'Got this season's fixtures done yet?' George asked.

'Yes and no,' replied Brian. 'Some clubs haven't replied yet, and mid-week evening games are always a problem. The depot team want to start at 5 o'clock, before they go home from work. We can't possibly get there by then unless we just take schoolboys . . .'

'And get a hammering like last year,' remembered George who'd left his silaging to play and taken none for 48.

'There's a couple of gaps in July just before our East Anglia tour. I'll leave the second one blank—keeps the wives happy if there's a Sunday free before we take their menfolk away for four days.'

'What are you going to do about the August bank holiday Monday?' asked Arthur.

'Domestic game, best really, saves us driving any distance, brings everyone in.'

'And you can get the subscriptions from those who haven't paid yet, if they're actually getting a game,' added Arthur.

'Well, anyway, you've enough to keep you busy for the rest of January,' summed up George as they wandered up to the pub to continue drinking the New Year in.

'Sally, pass me the paper again—and the marmalade—I want to read that ad. offering a roller.' Brian spread his toast and drank his coffee while reading, in the

February issue of *The Cricketer*, that a motor-roller was for sale from a nearby town club. He had long wanted a motor-roller for Cricket St Bede. The sort of fixtures they were securing nowadays called for really good wickets. The club owed it to their opponents. Brian finished his breakfast and got on the 'phone.

'That mower you're advertising. Has it gone? No? Good! Can you tell me its weight? Who are the makers? Have you got the model number? You'll look it up? You say it's just had a reconditioned engine. I'll want to be assured we can get spares for it. What do you want for it? I'd need to come and see it of course.'

Brian had a word with the groundsman at school who told him to ring the local agents for the makers once he had the model number. They would know about spares and tell him what they thought was a fair price.

'Probably going to look at a motor-roller on Saturday,' he told the Vth form, only too ready to take time off from studying Cromwell.

'Has it a side-valve engine?' asked a car enthusiast who hoped to be in the school eleven.

The class was away—safely launched on cricket until the bell went. 'We're not all Rachel Heyhoe-Flints, sir,' said a bored girl whose sympathies were very much with Cromwell who had banned cricket in Ireland.

'Rachel Heyhoe-Flint for captain—that'll make 'em grovel!' (*Cartoon by Giles, London Express Service*)

On Saturday Brian and Pat, an airline pilot in the club, drove off to view the motor-roller.

'I'd like you to start it up for us,' Pat asked the groundsman at the club. He listened, thinking how quiet the engine was.

'Rev it up a little would you?' Pat turned to Brian. 'There doesn't seem to be any smoke from the exhaust.' The groundsman stopped the engine. 'I want to take the oil filter cap off.' Pat satisfied himself that the engine was free of oil-leaks and that the cooling system was sound.

'Will we have to spend much on it?' Brian asked.

'Nothing major, only plugs and points.' Pat spoke again to the groundsman. 'She'll do,' he concluded.

'I suggest our secretary offers you £250, and we'll arrange a low-loader to take her away.' The deal was made, and the village club owned a motor-roller. February had been an eventful month.

Brian spent one Sunday afternoon in March calling on the ladies. 'There are worse ways of spending a Sunday afternoon,' he would say to some, or more gallantly, 'if there's a better way of passing a winter Sunday afternoon, I haven't heard of it.' The ladies were being asked to do the teas. Brian ensured that no one did it more than once a season. His visits were intended to get their agreement and to find out on what dates they were not available because of alternative attractions such as holidays, jumble sales and weddings.

Once he had his 'availability' list, Brian had to work out his pairs. 'Can't put Irene and Peggy together,' he said to Sally, 'they'll both want to make the cakes and neither do the sandwiches.'

'Worse than that', replied Sally, 'Irene's cakes are always the ones left to the end at the Conservative Produce Stall, and Peggy's are always the first to go.'

'Mustn't put Fred's wife on for the Tiddingly match; need our strongest team and Fred won't be playing.'

When Brian had got his pairs matched to his liking he turned to the ground-rota list. This consisted of allocating players to help Alf, the groundsman. They were expected to help one evening a week, turn up at eleven o'clock on the morning of the match, sweep the wicket, paint the lines, put out boundary flags, assemble the sight-screen, cut the out-field, put up the score-board and generally assist Alf. At the end of the game, the process was (mostly) reversed.

Brian had to bear several points in mind—just like the husbands of the tea-ladies, ground-assistants had to be assured of a game. You didn't ask Sidney to work a split-shift on the ground, from eleven to two-thirty and seven to seven-thirty, and sit on the benches in between. It meant that Sidney did his ground duty against Ravenshurst. The miracle about Ravenshurst was that they kept going year after year. They always brought a weak side, usually one short, and 80 was a good score.

'What keeps the Ravenshursts of this world going, Sally?' Brian asked.

'Jack Erskine and his wife,' she replied. 'It's a two-man band. She does all the teas for the summer, he prepares the wickets. Take them away, and Ravenshurst would fold up.'

Brian got back to his ground-assistants. Some men you put on duty the same day as their wives did the tea. Others wanted different days because of minding the children. The students and schoolboys in the club had to do their turn in July and August when exams were over.

Brian always went away for a week in April. The fixture card was printed and the paperwork for the season had been done. There was a breathing-space before the

The third Sunday in April (*Cartoon by Michael Bird*)

final run-in to the season. He and Sally would go to Norfolk and find a quiet pub which did bed-and-breakfast, explore National Trust properties before the tourist rush and walk along empty, bracing beaches. On the drive home they would stop to inspect one or two village grounds. Brian would comment disparagingly on the track or the out-field; occasionally he picked up an idea. There had been a dark green score-board which showed up the numbers better and he had been glad to copy that when he got home.

The third Sunday in April was the club's work-day. Brian reckoned to get all the players out. Skills had long been attributed, logically or otherwise. Sidney, a computer systems analyst, knew how to do the carpentry jobs. George, the farmer, cut the out-field. Peter, the lorry driver, oiled the bats. Pat, the airline pilot, helped Alf to apply some summer fertiliser and work it into the soil. John, the bank clerk, cleaned the pads.

Everyone recognised that Alf was the man in charge. He earned his living as a traveller. He dealt in a range of goods which could be classed as necessities rather than luxuries. He was well-known in his territory and had no difficulty in getting business. Alf could always find the time to work on the square—cutting and rolling, turfing and seeding, watering and weeding. As Brian watched him, he realised for the umpteenth time that men like Alf were a dying breed. Who would prepare the wickets of the 1990s?

'They'll probably all be artificial by then.'

'Think so?' said John. 'What price a leg-break bowler like me?' John's leg-breaks were a conspiratorial secret which he shared with no one else. Certainly, they remained undetected and there was little fear in opponents' hearts when John came on to bowl, setting his field with deliberation. Brian, who kept wicket, could always spot them because he had long ago decided there was nothing to spot.

With the arrival of May it was time to get a side out. Postage was becoming an expensive business. Brian could remember when he sent cards off to nearly all the team. Nowadays he economised. Players who were reliable and worth a place in any company got a permanent card from Brian. It carried the imposing sentence: 'This entitles you to play in all 1st XI matches during the season. It is your responsibility to inform the secretary if you are unavailable.'

Those members who didn't take Brian too seriously compared his permanent cards to Access cards, season tickets, and even luncheon vouchers. Brian issued eight of them. It meant he had only three places to offer to other members, which could become embarrassing when the students and schoolboys became available. Luckily, that was holiday time and the farmers' busy period. 'It'll work out; it always does,' he remarked, as the cards were dispatched and the season launched.

The village always had a prestige match in June. Brian thought it good for the club image. 'Ravenshurst and Fauxton are all very well,' he would say, 'but let's put ourselves on the map occasionally.'

One June the map was so far-flung that some members looked at an atlas to see where Brian had got the opposition from.

'Bermuda,' he announced. 'Some clubs there are sending a team over to tour and they advertised for fixtures.'

'Brian's overdone it this time,' was the general feeling. 'You can't expect a village to play that sort of opposition.'

The team from Bermuda arrived bearing gifts; a message of greeting from a local mayor and presentation ties. The village gave them lunch, tea and the local beer. Four hundred and twenty-one runs were scored by the two sides and the village won by the odd run.

'See you next year on our side of the pond,' shouted the visitors as the mini-bus pulled out of the pub yard.

'Anytime,' replied the villagers.

'Trouble is,' added John, 'who's going to pay?'

'It'll soon be much cheaper than your Dutch tour, Brian,' said Pat, 'watch those cut-price Atlantic fares.'

Brian dreamt that night of the Pacific route to Australia via Bermuda. The village had beaten New South Wales. Even Kerry Packer was interested in some of the players.

In July Cricket St Bede always went on tour. Numbers were the main problem. They chopped and changed by ones and twos as unexpected players became available and others dropped out. Wives and girl-friends changed their plans. Brian always made a firm booking of accommodation at a college hostel and hoped the final numbers would be approximate.

A few days before the party set out there was a pre-tour meeting in the pub.

'The main business is to sort out whose cars go. I think it would be fair if all passengers paid drivers three pounds towards petrol costs on the tour.' Brian was assertive, playing the schoolmaster-role. The players accepted it. They knew he ran an efficient tour, while he knew it was the only holiday in the year for some of them. It was important to balance efficiency with friendliness.

Each morning on the tour Brian would make announcements at breakfast. 'We're expected at Lyfield for an 11.30 start. Would players meet their drivers in the car park at 10 o'clock. George, would you take the club kit in your Land-rover? I think that Martin, our skipper, wants to say a word or two about who is standing down from today's game. Tomorrow's opponents, Eggleston, want to know lunch and tea numbers. I promised to 'phone them. Can I have a show of hands of those who will be with us?'

On the last evening of the tour, the club gave Brian a book token. 'Thanks for all your arrangements,' said Martin. 'It doesn't go unappreciated.'

August was a fairly slack month. Farming took priority and evening games were over for the year. Brian could sit back and watch the club's affairs run smoothly.

He and Sally disappeared for ten days and a youngster acted as assistant secretary.

'Grooming him for the job?' asked Martin. 'He'll have to wait as long as Edward VII had to.'

'No way,' said Brian. 'My twenty-year stint is up this December. I'll be asking you to propose a new secretary. Can't go on for ever, you know.'

The last game of the season happened on the last Sunday in September. Play had to end at 5.30 because the sun cast long shadows straight down the wicket. Batting was impossible at the bottom end. The village needed 8 to win against Tellfield. Peter faced the last over with Arthur in support at the other end. Two balls went by harmlessly outside the off-stump. The third missed both Peter and the Tellfield wicket-keeper. 'Two there,' called Arthur as they scrambled a couple of byes. A cloud moved towards the sun. It might be in time to give Peter a sight of the ball. He asked for guard again to give the cloud and himself a chance, and scratched his mark fussily rather than accurately, pulling his cap down even more over his left eye. The fourth ball appeared from nowhere. Peter played down the line and length and killed it. The cloud came nearer to his defence. He walked up to Arthur, patting the wicket involuntarily as he went.

'Settle for a draw?' he queried.

'Best now, I think,' said his partner, 'looks better in the press. "Tellfield held to a draw in last match."'

The sun played his last card of the season as he hung low and blindingly over the fifth ball of the over. It was a slower ball. Peter picked it up and kept it out of his wickets.

The cloud moved into position, in front of the sun. Tellfield's fast bowler went back to his mark for the last time for eight months. Cricket St Bede players came out of the changing-room in various stages of dress. Suddenly, Peter could see bowler and ball again. Normal play was resumed.

'Have a go,' he found himself saying as the final ball came down.

Peter connected with a loose ball outside the leg stump. The stroke was agricultural but who cared? The ball soared over square-leg to the short on-side boundary for six. The village had won the last match of the season.

Brian and Alf asked for help, willingly given after the final game. By 6.30 the ground was staked and roped, boundary flags stored away, score-board braced for the winter storms, seats put away in the barn.

'Want a hand with the rest of the jobs tomorrow night?' asked George.

'If you would, please,' replied Brian. 'We'll need to get a selective weedkiller out too,' added Alf, 'and do some spiking.'

'Last year running the show then?' asked Arthur.

'Last year,' said Brian.

The committee met in October. Colonel Crampton took the chair.

'Have we any apologies, Mr Secretary? Well, then, I ask members to receive the

The last game of the season (*Cartoon by Michael Bird*)

Minutes of the last meeting which have already been circulated. May I take these as an accurate record of what took place?'

The meeting followed the well-worn formula. The ground sub-committee report was presented—the table had been covered with grass seed and a top dressing of loam and fertiliser. The finance sub-committee report showed £210 in the ordinary account.

'Have we paid for the motor-roller, Mr Chairman?' asked George.

'Yes,' Arthur the treasurer replied, and added, 'I think the committee would like to know that I have £200 from the district council and £100 from the parish council towards our roller and our new tractor. And we shall be calling in the draw tickets at the dinner next month.'

Colonel Crampton turned to the dinner sub-committee for its report. By 10.30 the meeting was over.

'Who's this speaker chap you've got for the dinner, Brian?' asked Martin in the Bat and Ball.

'Commentator, played a little first-class cricket, knows how to tell a story—I've heard him before. It'll be a good evening.'

Over the years the club had alternated between having the November dinner as a self-help occasion in the village hall and as a more expensive celebration at one of the nearby town hotels. This year they had decided on the hall. The club silver was on the top table—the Festival of Britain Cup, the cup for competition against Lessingham, and a splendid trophy donated some years earlier and awarded to the best all-rounder of the season. The club flag hung from the rafters. Colonel Crampton took the chair. Vice-presidents and playing-members with their ladies and guests sat down to grapefruit, roast turkey, and peach melba. The guest speaker was a success, especially when he told the one about the village cricketer who turned up at Old Trafford with his kit.

The club had its Annual General Meeting in December. It broke up the winter, and gave the new committee time to get things planned. Brian got the agenda out at the beginning of the month, the Minutes of the last Annual General Meeting, reports from captain, secretary and treasurer, election of office-bearers. There was a good tradition of turning up unless it was a really bad night.

Thirty-two members, including several youngsters who might learn how a club ran behind the scenes, were present. Martin, the captain, complimented the club on winning more than half its matches. He was especially pleased that Herbert, one of the younger players from the side, had gone up to Cambridge and got a 'Blue'. Brian, in his report, thanked all who had contributed to the season's success. Arthur, the treasurer, threatened in future years to 'name from the chair' those who had not yet paid their subscriptions.

The meeting turned to the election of office-bearers.

'I call for nominations for the post of secretary,' said the chairman.

'Better be Brian again; I'll propose Brian,' said John.

'Any other nominations?'

'So, it's your twenty-first year now, is it?' said George to Brian on the way home from the Bat and Ball afterwards.

'Have a good Christmas. See you on New Year's Eve.'

BIBLIOGRAPHY

For 200 years village cricket matches have been reported in local newspapers. In the eighteenth century, those villages in the south-east whose cricket was linked with betting got much advance publicity for their forthcoming matches though rather less attention was given to the matches themselves. Nineteenth-century village cricket was often reported at considerable length, depending on the enthusiasm of the local correspondent. Village cricket in the twentieth century, and especially since 1945, is reported in nearly all provincial newspapers serving a small local area. Interested readers should consult their County Record Offices or the British Museum newspaper section at Colindale about the whereabouts of papers in which they might be interested. I have mentioned in the course of this book those I have used. They are a fraction of the whole!

The Cricketer, founded in 1921, has devoted space to village cricket over the years, more especially in the 1970s.

I consulted the books listed below. All of them make some reference to village cricket, either in fact or fiction. Many are out of print and prospective readers may need to approach their local libraries to obtain them:

Allen, Phoebe. *The Cricket Club* (1884)
Altham, H. S. and Swanton, E. W. *A History of Cricket* (1926)
Arlott, John. *From Hambledon to Lords* (1975)
Ashley-Cooper, F. S. *The Hambledon Cricket Chronicle* (1923)
Blunden, E. C. *English Villages* (1941)
Bowen, Roland. *Cricket: a History* (1970)
Broadribb, Gerald. *The English Game: a Cricket Anthology* (1948)
Brookes, Christopher. *English Cricket* (1978)
Buckley, G. B. *Fresh Light on Eighteenth-century Cricket* (1935); *Fresh Light on pre-Victorian Cricket* (1937)
Cardus, Neville. *English Cricket* (1945)
Colloms, Brenda. *Victorian Country Parsons* (1977)
'Country Vicar'. *Happy Cricketer* (1946)
De Sélincourt, Hugh. *The Cricket Match* (1924); *The Game of the Season* (1931); *'Over!'* (1932); *The Saturday Match* (1937)
Dickens, Charles. *Martin Chuzzlewit* (1843); *Pickwick Papers* (1836); *Sunday*

Under Three Heads (1836)
Fogg, John. *The Haig Book of Village Cricket* (1972)
Forrest, A. J. *Village Cricket* (1957)
Gibbs, J. A. *A Cotswold Village* (1898)
Goldsmith, John. *Hambledon: the Biography of a Hampshire Village* (1971)
Goulstone, John. *Early Club and Village Cricket* (1972)
Home, Michael. *Autumn Fields* (1944)
Kay, John. *Cricket in the Leagues* (1970)
Lillywhite, Frederick. *Scores and Biographies*, vols i-iv (1862-3)
Looker, S. J. (ed.) *Cricket: an Anthology* (1925)
Lucas, E. V. *The Hambledon Men* (1907)
Lyon, M. D. *A Village Match and After* (1929)
Macdonnell, A. G. *England, Their England* (1933)
Meredith, George. *Diana of the Crossways* (1885); *Evan Harrington* (1861); *The Adventures of Harry Richmond* (1871)
Middleton, C. H. *Village Memories* (1941)
Mitford, Mary. *Our Village* (1824)
Moore, John. *Brensham Village* (1946); *The Countryman's England* (1939)
Nyren, John. *The Young Cricketer's Tutor* (1833)
Parker, Eric (ed.) *The Cricketer's Weekend Book* (1952)
Parker, John. *The Village Cricket Match* (1977)
Parker, John. *Test Time at Tillingford* (1979)
Pycroft, James. *Elkerton Rectory* (1860); *The Cricket Field* (1851); *The Cricket Tutor* (1862)
Rea, Findlay and Scanlan, Tom (eds.) *Haig Village Cricket Annuals* (1974-8)
Rheinberg, Netta. *Fairplay* (1975)
Ross, Alan (ed.) *The Cricketer's Companion* (1960)
Sherriff, R. C. *Badger's Green* (1930)
Simons, E. N. *Friendly Eleven* (1950)
Stevenson, N. L. *Play!* (1946)
Young, R. S. *Cricket on the Green* (1947)
Wells, H. G. *Certain Personal Matters* (1898)

Histories of village cricket clubs are an important source. They are usually privately printed but may be traced in *A Bibliography of Cricket* (1977) compiled by E. W. Padwick. This important volume lists over 8,000 books, brochures, pamphlets and periodicals covering the whole range of cricket, published up to the end of 1973. Among especially well-written village cricket histories which I read were these:

A Century at Blackheath
Earlswood, 1876-1976

Great Oakley Cricket (H. and E. Bagshaw)
Henfield C.C. Bi-centenary, 1971
Ifield, 1804-1954
The History of Lascelles Hall (ed. E. A. Wood)
The History of Meopham C.C. (W. Gunyon)
A History of Seaton Carew C.C., 1829-1965 (D. Hornby)
A Record of Cricket in St Boswells (J. K. Ballantyne)
Smuggler's Village: the Story of Rottingdean (Henry Blyth)
Stapleton C.C. 1863-1963
Thornbury C.C., Centenary Handbook, 1871-1971 (ed. S. Canynge Caple)
Whitbread Village Cricket Booklet (1979)

ACKNOWLEDGEMENTS

I am indebted to a great many people. I hope all those who entertained me, answered letters and lent me material will accept my warmest thanks. Among those to whom I am particularly grateful for help are the following:

Messrs W. G. Anderson; Ken Beaumont; Henry Blyth; Maurice Bolitho; Michael Bradford; J. F. Burrell; R. H. Butcher; Charles Clarke; N. M. Collar; Bernard Cook; F. J. Cooke; Aubrey Davey; H. J. Edwards; Humphrey Elcock; Peter Glover; Stephen Green; William Gunyon; George Harbottle; D. Hayward; Roger Heavens; D. Hornby; Alan Howick; Brian Jones; David Lanford; James Leven; David Luke; John Macdonald; Sam McGowan; Richard Malone; Fred Matthews; F. G. Mayston; F. Mitchell; Howard Naish; Arthur Pattendon; A. L. Robinson; Ray Robinson; G. R. Rogers; D. A. Skinner; H. Slater; James Small; Roy Smith; K. Stoddart; W. B. Swan; M. J. Taylor; W. E. Townsend; R. B. Warsop; Stan Welland; Gordon Wood; Anthony Woodhouse; Peter Worsley; Ron Yeomans; together with Mrs Anne Fisher; Mrs James Lawrence; The Earl of Mansfield; Miss Netta Rheinberg; Mrs A. C. Somerset; and Major P. C. T. Wildash.

I am also grateful to my friend Max Reese, historian and sports writer *extraordinaire*, who read the entire manuscript and saved it (as the phrase goes) from many infelicities of style, to Norman Lilley of the Queensway Studios, Thame, who performed photographic wonders on many very old and faded prints, and to Mrs Joyce Hewitt and my daughter, Gillian, for their typing.

Most of the illustrations, other than those individually acknowledged, have been taken from photographs in the possession of clubs. My friend Nicolas Bentley had promised to do some new work for this book but died just before starting the drawings; I have included the only two—so far as I know—which he ever did upon cricket. I am also grateful for the original work of Michael Bird in Chapter 11 and for Jill Allonby's chapter-end decorations.

INDEX